Samsung® Galaxy S® 4
FOR

DUMMIES®

Portable Edition

by Bill Hughes

FOR

DUMMIES®

A Wiley Brand

Samsung® Galaxy S® 4 For Dummies,® Portable Edition

Published by:
John Wiley & Sons, Inc.
111 River Street
Hoboken, NJ 07030-5774
www.wiley.com

Copyright © 2013 by John Wiley & Sons, Inc., Hoboken, New Jersey

Published simultaneously in Canada

No part of this publication may be reproduced, stored in a retrieval system or transmitted in any form or by any means, electronic, mechanical, photocopying, recording, scanning or otherwise, except as permitted under Sections 107 or 108 of the 1976 United States Copyright Act, without the prior written permission of the Publisher. Requests to the Publisher for permission should be addressed to the Permissions Department, John Wiley & Sons, Inc., 111 River Street, Hoboken, NJ 07030, (201) 748-6011, fax (201) 748-6008, or online at http://www.wiley.com/go/permissions.

Trademarks: Wiley, For Dummies, the Dummies Man logo, Dummies.com, Making Everything Easier, and related trade dress are trademarks or registered trademarks of John Wiley & Sons, Inc. and may not be used without written permission. Samsung and Galaxy S are registered trademarks of Samsung Electronics Co. Ltd. All other trademarks are the property of their respective owners. John Wiley & Sons, Inc. is not associated with any product or vendor mentioned in this book.

For general information on our other products and services, please contact our Customer Care Department within the U.S. at 877-762-2974, outside the U.S. at 317-572-3993, or fax 317-572-4002.

For technical support, please visit www.wiley.com/techsupport.

Wiley publishes in a variety of print and electronic formats and by print-on-demand. Some material included with standard print versions of this book may not be included in e-books or in print-on-demand. If this book refers to media such as a CD or DVD that is not included in the version you pur-chased, you may download this material at http://booksupport.wiley.com. For more information about Wiley products, visit www.wiley.com.

ISBN 978-1-118-79396-1

Manufactured in the United States of America

10 9 8 7 6 5 4 3 2 1

Contents at a Glance

Table of Contents

Chapter 8: Shopping in the Google Play Store.......103

Chapter 9: Sharing Pictures and Video 119

Chapter 10: Ten Ways to Make Your Phone Secure..........................131

Publisher's Acknowledgments

We're proud of this book; please send us your comments at `http://dummies.custhelp.com`. For other comments, please contact our Customer Care Department within the U.S. at 877-762-2974, outside the U.S. at 317-572-3993, or fax 317-572-4002.

Some of the people who helped bring this book to market include the following:

Acquisitions, Editorial, and Media Development

Project Editor: Linda Morris

Executive Editor: Katie Mohr

Editorial Manager: Jodi Jensen

Editorial Assistant: Annie Sullivan

Sr. Editorial Assistant: Cherie Case

Cover photo: ©iStockphoto.com/ quavondo; Samsung Galaxy S 4 courtesy of Samsung

Composition Services

Sr. Project Coordinator: Kristie Rees

Layout and Graphics: Jennifer Goldsmith

Proofreader: Jessica Kramer

Indexer: Potomac Indexing, LLC

Publishing and Editorial for Technology Dummies

Richard Swadley, Vice President and Executive Group Publisher

Andy Cummings, Vice President and Publisher

Mary Bednarek, Executive Acquisitions Director

Mary C. Corder, Editorial Director

Publishing for Consumer Dummies

Kathleen Nebenhaus, Vice President and Executive Publisher

Composition Services

Debbie Stailey, Director of Composition Services

Introduction

*T*he Samsung Galaxy S 4 is a powerful smartphone, perhaps the most powerful phone ever sold. As of the publication of this book, the Galaxy S 4 is the standard against which all other Android-based phones are measured.

All Galaxy S phones use Google's Android platform. This is the equivalent of different brands of PCs all being based upon Microsoft's Windows operating system. Although there are some differences in how the operating system appears when you turn on your PC for the first time, the experience is largely similar whether the PC comes from Dell or from HP.

The good news is that the Android platform has proven to be widely popular, even more successful than Google originally expected when it first announced it in November of 2007. More people are using Android-based phones, and more third parties are writing applications. This is good news because it offers you more options for applications (more on this in Chapter 8 on the Play Store, where you buy applications).

Smartphones are getting smarter all the time, and the Galaxy S 4 is one of the smartest. However, just because you've used a smartphone in the past doesn't mean you should expect to use your new Galaxy S 4 without a bit of guidance.

That's where this book comes in. This book is a hands-on guide to getting the most out of your Galaxy S 4.

About This Book

This book is a reference — you don't have to read it from beginning to end to get all you need out of it. The information is clearly organized and easy to access. You don't need thick glasses to understand this book. This book helps you figure out what you want to do — and then tells you how to do it in plain English.

I don't use many conventions in this book, but here are a few you should know about:

- ✔ Whenever I introduce a new term, I put it in *italics* and define it shortly thereafter (often in parentheses).

✔ I use **bold** for the action parts of numbered steps, so you can easily see what you're supposed to do.

✔ I use `monofont` for web addresses and e-mail addresses, so they stand out from the surrounding text. If you're reading this as an e-book, these links are live and clickable.

Foolish Assumptions

You know what they say about assuming, so I don't do much of it in this book. But I do make a few assumptions about you:

✔ **You have a Galaxy S 4 phone.** You may be thinking about buying a Galaxy S 4 phone, but my money's on your already owning one. After all, getting your hands on the phone is the best part!

✔ **You're not totally new to cellphones.** You know that your Galaxy S 4 phone is capable of doing more than the average cellphone, and you're eager to find out what your phone can do.

✔ **You've used a computer.** You don't have to be a computer expert, but you at least know how to check your e-mail and surf the web.

Icons Used in This Book

Throughout this book, I used *icons* (little pictures in the margin) to draw your attention to various types of information. Here's a key to what those icons mean:

This whole book is like one series of tips. When I share especially useful tips and tricks, I mark them with the Tip icon.

This book is a reference, which means you don't have to commit it to memory — there is no test at the end. But once in a while, I do tell you things that are so important that I think you should remember them, and when I do, I mark them with the Remember icon.

Whenever you may do something that could cause a major headache, I warn you with the, er, Warning icon.

When you see this icon, you'll find interesting but optional information that you can skip if you like.

1

Exploring the Galaxy

In This Chapter

▶ Reviewing the basic capabilities of just about any cellphone

▶ Understanding what sets smartphones apart

▶ Mapping out what makes Samsung Galaxy S 4 phones so cool

*W*hether you want just the basics from a phone (make and take phone calls, customize your ringtone, take some pictures, maybe use a Bluetooth headset) or you want your phone to always be by your side (a tool for multiple uses throughout your day), you can make that happen. In this chapter, I outline all the things your phone can do — from the basics, to what makes Galaxy S 4 phones different from the rest. Throughout the remainder of the book, I walk you through the steps to get your phone doing what makes you the happiest.

Discovering the Basics of Your Phone

All cellphones on the market today include basic functions, and even some entry-level phones are a little more sophisticated. Of course, Samsung includes all basic functions on the Galaxy S 4 model. In addition to making and taking calls (see Chapter 3) and sending and receiving texts (see Chapter 4), the Galaxy S 4 sports the following basic features:

  ✔ **13MP digital camera:** This resolution is more than enough for posting good-quality images on the Internet and even having 4" x 6" prints made.

- **Ringtones:** You can replace the standard ringtone with custom ringtones that you download to your phone. You can also specify different rings for different numbers.

- **Bluetooth:** The Galaxy S 4 phone supports stereo and standard Bluetooth devices.

- **High-resolution screen:** The Galaxy S 4 phone offers one of the highest-resolution touchscreens on the market (1920×1080 pixels).

- **Capacitive touchscreen:** The Galaxy S 4 phone offers a very slick touchscreen that's sensitive enough to allow you to interact with the screen accurately, but not so sensitive that it's hard to manage. In addition, it has an optional setting that steps up the sensitivity in case you need to use your phone while wearing gloves.

Taking Your Phone to the Next Level: The Smartphone Features

In addition to the basic capabilities of any entry-level cellphone, the Galaxy S 4 phone, which is based upon the popular Android platform, has capabilities associated with other smartphones, such as the Apple iPhone and the phones based upon Windows Phone 8:

- **Internet access:** Access websites through a web browser on your phone.

- **Photos:** The phone comes with a camera, but also the ability to manage photos.

- **Wireless e-mail:** Send and receive e-mail from your phone.

- **Multimedia:** Play music and videos on your phone.

- **Contact Manager:** The Galaxy S 4 phone lets you take shortcuts to avoid having to enter someone's ten-digit number each time you want to call or text that person. In fact, the Contact Manager has the ability to track all the numbers that your contacts might have plus their e-mail addresses and photos. On top of that, it can synchronize with the contact manager on both your personal and work PCs.

- **Digital camcorder:** The Galaxy S 4 phone comes with a built-in digital camcorder that records at a resolution that you can set, including HD.

✔ **Mapping and directions:** The Galaxy S 4 phone uses the GPS (Global Positioning System) in your phone to tell you where you are, find local services that you need, and give you directions to where you want to go.

✔ **Business applications:** The Galaxy S 4 can keep you productive while you're away from the office.

I go into each of these capabilities in greater detail in the following sections.

Internet access

Until a few years ago, the only way to access the Internet when you were away from a desk was with a laptop. Smartphones are a great alternative to laptops because they're small, convenient, and ready to launch their web browsers right away. Even more important, when you have a smartphone, you can access the Internet wherever you are — whether Wi-Fi is available or not.

The drawback to smartphones, however, is that their screen size is smaller than even the most basic laptop screen. The pixel resolution is there, but the raw real estate of the screen is not. Plus, image-heavy websites can take a long time to load. To accommodate this problem, more websites are adding mobile versions. These sites are slimmed-down versions of their main sites with fewer images but similar access to information. These site names usually begin with m or mobile, such as m.yahoo.com.

Figure 1-1 shows the regular website for Refdesk.com on the left and its mobilized version on the right. The mobilized version has no pictures and is more vertically oriented.

On the Galaxy S 4 phone, you can use the mobile version of a website if you want, but if you prefer to use the standard website, you can pinch and stretch your way to get the information you want — see Chapter 2 for more information on pinching and stretching.

For more information on accessing the Internet from your Galaxy S 4 phone, turn to Chapter 7.

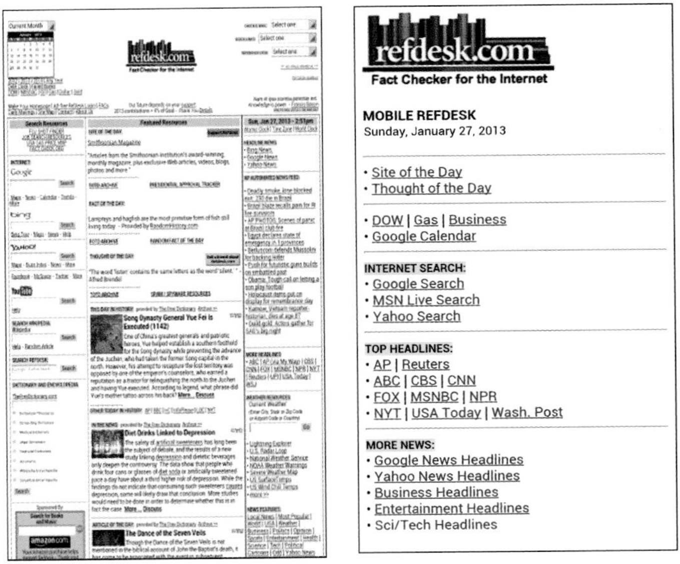

Figure 1-1: A mobile website is a slimmed-down version of the main site.

Photos

The image application on your phone helps you use the digital camera on your Galaxy S 4 phone to its full potential. Studies have found that cellphone users tend to snap a bunch of pictures within the first month of phone usage. After that, the photos sit on the phone (instead of being downloaded to a computer), and the picture-taking rate drops dramatically.

The Galaxy S 4 phone image management application is different. You can integrate your camera images into your home photo library, as well as photo-sharing sites such as Picasa and Flickr, with minimal effort.

For more on how to use the Photo applications, you can turn to Chapter 9.

Wireless e-mail

On your Galaxy smartphone, you can access your business and personal e-mail accounts, reading and sending e-mail messages on the go. Depending on your e-mail system, you might be able to sync so that when you delete an e-mail on your phone, the e-mail is deleted on your computer at the same time so you don't have to read the same messages on your phone and your computer.

Chapter 5 covers setting up your business and personal e-mail accounts.

Multimedia

Some smartphones allow you to play music and videos on your phone in place of a dedicated MP3 or video player. On the Galaxy S 4 phone, you can use the applications that come with the phone, or you can download applications that offer these capabilities from the Play Store.

Customizing Your Phone with Games and Applications

Application developers — large and small — are working on the Android platform to offer a variety of applications and games for the Galaxy S 4 phone. Compared to most of the other smartphone platforms, Google imposes fewer restrictions on application developers regarding what is allowable. This freedom to develop resonates with many developers, resulting in a bonanza of application development on this platform.

As of this writing, more than 700,000 applications are available from Google's Play Store. For more information about downloading games and applications, turn to Chapter 8.

Downloading applications and games

Your phone comes with some very nice applications, but these might not take you as far as you want to go. You might also have some special interests, like philately or star-gazing, that neither Samsung nor your carrier felt would be of sufficient general interest to include on the phone. (Can you imagine?)

You phone also comes with preloaded *widgets,* which are smaller applications that serve a particular purpose, such as retrieving stock quotes or telling you how your phone's battery is feeling today. They reside on the extended Home screen and are instantly available.

Buying applications and games allows you to get additional capabilities and entertainment quickly, easily, and inexpensively. Ultimately, these make your phone, which is already a reflection of who you are, more personal as you add more capabilities.

What's cool about the Android platform

The Samsung Galaxy S 4 phone is the top-of-the-line Android phone. That means that any application developed for an Android phone will run to its full capability. This is significant because one of the founding principles in the creation of the Android platform is to create an environment where application developers can be as creative as possible without an oppressive organization dictating what can and cannot be sold (as long as it's within the law, of course). This has inspired many of the best applications developers to go with Android first.

On top of that, Android is designed to run multiple applications at once. Other smartphone platforms have added this capability, but Android is designed for you to be able to jump quickly among multiple apps that you're running — and that makes your experience that much smoother.

Understanding How Your Cellular Carrier Bills You

In the United States, most cellular companies sell phones at a significant discount when you sign up for a service agreement. And most cellular companies offer discounts on phones when you want to upgrade to something newer (as long as you also sign up for another couple of years of service). So, it's not surprising that most people buy their phones directly from cellular companies.

If your new Galaxy S 4 phone device is an upgrade from an older phone, you might have a service plan that was suitable for your last phone but isn't so great anymore. If this is your first cellphone (ever, or with this particular carrier), you might start with an entry-level plan, thinking you don't need "that many minutes," only to find that you and your phone are inseparable, and you need a better plan. The good news is that most cellular carriers allow you to change your service plan.

Most cellular service plans have three components of usage:

- ✔ Voice
- ✔ Text
- ✔ Data

In the following sections, I walk you through each of these components and how they affect using your Galaxy S 4.

Voice usage

Voice usage is the most common, costly, and complex element of most service plans. Cellular providers typically offer plans with a certain number of anytime minutes and a certain number of night/weekend minutes. Some providers offer plans with reduced rates (or even free calls) to frequently called numbers, to other cellphones with the same cellular provider, or to other cellphones in general. If you talk a lot, you might be able to opt for an unlimited voice plan (for domestic calls only).

At its core, a Galaxy S 4 phone device is, obviously, a phone. In the early days of smartphones, manufacturers were stung by the criticism that smartphones weren't as easy to use as traditional cellphones. Indeed, you do have to bring up the phone screen to make a call (more on making and receiving calls in Chapter 3). As an improvement, Samsung has made sure that the screen used to make calls is only one click away from the Home screen.

 If keeping track of minutes is important to you and your calling plan, be mindful of all those e-mails and social network updates that prompt you to call someone right away. You might be tempted to make more calls than you did with your old (dumb) cellular phone.

Text usage

A texting "bundle" is an add-on to your voice plan. Some service plans include unlimited texting; others offer a certain number of text messages for a flat rate. For example, maybe you pay an additional $5 per month to get 200 free text messages — meaning that combined, you can send and receive a *total* of 200 messages per month. If you go over that limit, you pay a certain amount per message (usually more for text messages you send than for those you receive).

As with voice, the Galaxy S 4 phone makes it very convenient to text, making it more likely that you'll use this service and end up using more texts than you expect. However, nothing obligates you to buy a texting plan.

My advice is to get at least some texting capability, but be ready to decide if you want to pay for more or stay with a minimal plan and budget your texts.

Data usage

Although getting texting may be optional, access to the Internet is essential to get the full experience of your Galaxy S 4 phone. The Internet is where you access the capabilities that make the Galaxy S 4 phone so special. Some cellular carriers may let you use the phone on their network without a data plan. I cannot imagine why you would want to do that. Although your phone will supplement the coverage you get from your cellular carrier with Wi-Fi, you really need to have a data plan from your cellular carrier to get the most value out of your investment in your phone. There's just no getting around it.

Most cellular companies price Internet access with usage increments measured in the hundreds of megabytes (MB), but more often in gigabytes (GB).

As of this writing, Sprint makes it easy by only offering unlimited data. This is good news: As you customize your phone to keep up with your friends and access your favorite sites, the cost of access won't increase.

Other carriers offer an unlimited option, but at a higher price. It is a challenge to figure out how much data you are going to need without going over the limit and paying a usage penalty. Some carriers try to help you by giving you some tools to estimate your usage by estimating the number of e-mails, web pages, or multimedia files you plan to download.

These are iffy. One option is to go with the lowest increment of data, unless you plan to be downloading a large number of videos, but using some of the tools I cover later to see how much data you are actually using.

Another school of thought is to go for an increment of data larger than you think you'll need. After you have some experience with how much data you actually use, you can call your carrier to scale back your usage if appropriate.

Don't blame me if you do not check your usage! It's easy to check and increase your usage, even mid-billing cycle.

Another consideration: Family plans

A popular option is to combine your usage of voice, text, and data with your family members. The family unit on the plan gets to share a fixed allotment of voice minutes, texts, and data. This works well, as long as a responsible person checks your usage during the billing period!

One final consideration: Web subscription fees

Don't forget that some web-based services charge subscription fees. For example, WeatherBug offers a consumer service that gives you weather conditions, but it also offers WeatherBug Pro that provides more information — with a monthly fee to subscribers. Yup, if you want WeatherBug Pro on your phone, you have to pay the piper. Some of these services can be billed through your cellular carrier (check first), but just make sure you're willing to pony up for the service.

Surviving Unboxing Day

When you turn on your phone the first time, it will ask you a series of questions and preferences to configure it. Frankly, they are trying to make this book unnecessary and put me out of business. The nerve!

The good folks at Samsung are well intentioned, but not every one of their customers with a Samsung Galaxy S 4 knows from day one whether she wants a Samsung account, what's a good name for her phone, or what the purpose of a drop box is, much less whether she wants to bother to sign up for one.

You can relax. I'll help you answer these questions, or, when appropriate, I refer you to the chapter within this book that helps you come up with your answer.

On the other hand, if your phone is already set up, you probably took a guess or skipped some questions. Maybe now you're rethinking some of your choices. No problem. You can go back and change any answer you gave and get your phone to behave the way you want.

The questions are as follows:

- ✓ **Screen 1: Language/Accessibility:** This option lets you select your language. The default is English for phones sold within the United States. Also, the phone has some special capabilities for individuals with disabilities. If you have a disability and think you might benefit, take a look at these options.

- ✓ **Screen 2: Wi-Fi:** Your phone automatically starts scanning for a Wi-Fi connection. You can always use the cellular connection when you are in cellular coverage, but if there is a Wi-Fi connection available, your phone will try to use this first. It is probably cheaper and may be faster than the cellular.

  At the same time, you may not want your phone to connect to the Wi-Fi access point with the best signal. It could be that the strongest signal is a fee-based service, whereas the next best signal is free. In any case, this page scans the available options and presents them to you. If you need to enter a password, you'll see the screen in Figure 1-2.

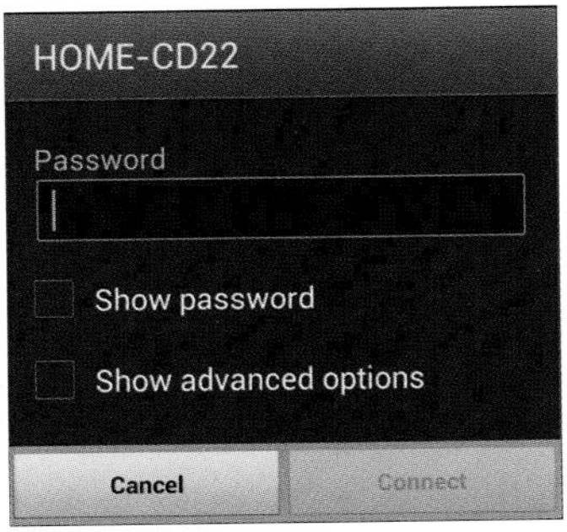

HOME-CD22

Password
|

☐ Show password

☐ Show advanced options

Cancel   Connect

Figure 1-2: The pop-up window for a Wi-Fi password.

If this is all too much to take in right now, feel free to skip to the next screen.

✔ **Screen 3: Date and Time:** This is easy. The default setting is to use the time and date that comes from the cellular network. Just tap on the next button and move on. This date and time from the cellular network is the most accurate information you will get, and you do not need to do anything other than be within cellular coverage now and again.

✔ **Screen 4: Sign up for a Samsung Account:** My advice is to skip this screen for now. The Samsung account offers you some nice things such as backing up your phone information and access to music, movies, and video. At the same time, there is so much more out there that it is best to forge ahead and leave this for another time.

✔ **Screen 5: Google Account Sign-up:** "Google account" means an e-mail account where the address ends in @gmail.com. If you already have an account on Gmail, enter your user ID and password here. If you do not have a Gmail account, I suggest waiting until you read Chapter 5. I recommend that you create a Gmail account, but it is best to go through some other steps first.

✔ **Screen 6: Location Options:** Your phone knowing your location and providing it to an application can be a sensitive issue.

If you are really worried about privacy and security, tap the green checkmarks on the screen and then tap the button that says Next. Selecting these options prevents applications from knowing where you are. This prevents you from getting directions and a large number of cool capabilities that are built into applications. The only folks who will know your location are the 911 dispatchers if you dial them.

If you are worried about your security, but may want to take advantage of some of the cool capabilities built into your phone, tap the right arrow key to move forward. Remember, you can choose on a case-by-case basis whether to share your location. I cover this more in Chapter 8.

✔ **Screen 7: Phone Ownership:** This screen asks you to enter your first and last name. You may ask why this is important at this point. It's not. If you have been able to navigate this far, you may be ready to tap in your first and last name. If not, just tap the right arrow. All will be fine.

✔ **Screen 8: Dropbox:** This is a generous offer, but what is it for? Dropbox is a service that allows you to store or transfer files online. If you need it, you can come back and take them up on it later. For now, just tap Skip.

✔ **Screen 9: Learn about key features:** If you think you don't need this book, go ahead and take this tour of all the new things you can do. If you think you might need this book in any way, shape, or form, tap the Next button. This screen is for setting up the coolest and the most sophisticated capabilities of the phone. I cover many of them in the course of this book. For now, skip this to get to the last screen.

✔ **Screen 10: Device Name:** When this screen comes up, you'll see a text box that has the model name. You can keep this name or you can choose to personalize it a bit. For example, you can change it to "Bill's Galaxy S 4" or "Indy at 425-555-1234." The purpose of this name is for connecting to a local data network, such as when you are pairing to a Bluetooth device. If this last sentence made no sense to you, don't worry about it. Tap Finish. In a moment, you see the Home screen, as shown in Figure 1-3.

Figure 1-3: The Home screen for the Samsung Galaxy S 4.

2

Getting Started
with Your S 4

*I*n this chapter, I fill you in on the basics of using your new Samsung Galaxy S 4. You start by turning on your phone. (I told you I was covering the basics!) I guide you through charging your phone and getting the most out of your phone's battery. Stick with me for a basic tour of your phone's buttons and other features. Then I end by telling you how to turn off your phone or put it in "sleep" mode.

Unless you're new to cellphones in general — and smartphones in particular — you might want to skip this chapter. If the term "smartphone" is foreign to you, you probably haven't used one before, and reading this chapter won't hurt. And, just so you know, a *smartphone* is just a cellular phone on which you can download and run applications that are better than what comes preloaded on a phone right out of the box.

First Things First: Turning On Your Phone

When you open the box of your new phone, the packaging will present you with your phone, wrapped in plastic, readily accessible. If you haven't already, take the phone out of the plastic bag and remove any protective covering material on the screen.

First things first. The On button is on the right side of the phone. You can see the symbol on the button in Figure 2-1. Press the On button for a second, and see whether it vibrates and the screen lights up. Hopefully, your phone arrived with enough electrical charge that you won't have to plug it in to an outlet right away. You can enjoy your new phone for the first day without having to charge it.

The On button

Figure 2-1: The On button on the phone.

The phones that you get at the stores of most cellular carriers usually come with the battery installed, partially charged, and registered with the network.

If the screen does light up, don't hold the On button too long, or the phone might turn off.

If the phone screen doesn't light up (rats), you need to charge the battery. Here's the rub: It's important to fully charge the battery for 24 hours, or at least overnight, so that it will last as long as possible. That means that you have to wait to use your beautiful new phone. Sorry.

Of course, it's possible that the battery needs to be inserted in the first place. To do this, you need to open the case. This isn't the end of the world, though. In fact, you should learn to do this sooner or later, anyway, so keep reading to see how.

Removing the Peel-Off Back for the Galaxy S 4

To expose the slots for the optional memory card, SIM card, and the battery slot, you remove the back by slipping a finger-nail under the back cover. There is a small slot to make this easier on the right side toward the top of the phone; see its location in Figure 2-2.

Don't use a sharp object, like a knife, to peel off the back of the phone. You might get away with that once or twice, but you'll end up scratching the plastic. If you have chewed your nails to the nubbins, ask someone with fingernails to do it for you — or use something plastic, like a credit card.

If you look at the bottom of the phone, there is something that looks like a nice, large slot that you can use to peel off the back of the phone. This is actually a micro-USB port where you connect your phone to be charged. Don't try to remove the back of the phone by using this port. If you stick a knife or something sharp in this port, you will probably damage the micro-USB port and no longer be able to charge your phone!

Open the cover here.

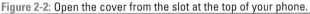

Figure 2-2: Open the cover from the slot at the top of your phone.

Without the back, you can see the insides of your phone, as shown in Figure 2-3.

From here, you can insert or remove the following components, as needed:

 ✔ The battery (you can't miss it).

 ✔ The MicroSD card to store files, music, and video.

 ✔ Your SIM card. (More on SIM cards in Chapter 6.)

In each case, look for a small engraving or printed image that shows you the correct orientation for the MicroSD card and the SIM card. It might be small and faint, but it's there!

Battery

SIM card

Memory card

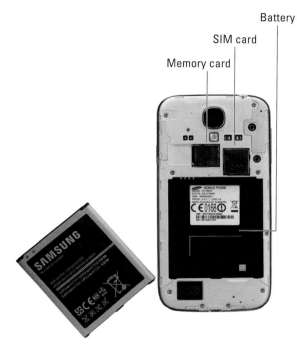

Figure 2-3: The insides of your phone.

Putting in and taking out the MicroSD card (Figure 2-4) is easy. You may want to practice, but be careful not to lose it. It is about the size of the fingernail on your little finger.

Figure 2-4: The MicroSD card.

To remove a MicroSD card from the port, push it in just a bit with your fingernail, and it will spring out like toast out of a toaster.

If you try to force the MicroSD card out simply by pulling it out, you will ruin the card.

You may have noticed that it is important to have fingernails with the Samsung Galaxy S 4. If you ever recommend the Galaxy S 4 to a friend, you may also want to suggest that she get a manicure beforehand.

Charging Your Phone and Managing Battery Life

Although you probably don't have to plug your phone into an outlet right away, the first time you do plug it in, allow it to charge overnight.

You'll hear all kinds of "battery lore" left over from earlier battery technologies. For example, lithium-ion (Li-ion) batteries don't have a "memory" like nickel-cadmium (NiCad) batteries did. And the Samsung Galaxy S 4 does use Li-ion batteries. That means that you don't have to be careful to allow the battery to fully discharge before recharging it.

Your phone comes with a two-piece battery charger (cable and the transformer), as shown in Figure 2-5.

Figure 2-5: The transformer and USB cable for charging your phone.

The cable has two ends: one end that plugs into the phone, and the other that's a standard USB connector. The phone end is a small connector called a micro USB that is used on some Samsung devices and is becoming the standard for charging cellphones and other small electronics, and for connecting them to computers.

To charge the phone, you have two choices:

✔ Plug the transformer into a wall socket and then plug the cable's USB plug into the USB receptacle in the transformer.

✔ Plug the USB on the cable into a USB port on your PC.

Then you plug the small end of the cable into the phone. The port is on the bottom of the phone. Make sure you push the little metal plug all the way in.

It doesn't really matter in what order you plug in things. However, if you use the USB port on a PC, the PC needs to be powered on for the phone to charge.

Unplug the transformer when you aren't charging your phone. A charger left plugged in will draw a small but continuous stream of power.

If your phone is Off when you're charging the battery, an image of a battery displays onscreen for a moment. The green portion of the battery indicates the amount of charge within the battery. You can get the image to reappear with a quick press of the Power button. This gives you the status of the battery without your having to turn on the phone.

If your phone is On, you see a small battery icon at the top of the screen showing how much charge is in the phone's battery. When the battery in the phone is fully charged, it vibrates to let you know that it's done and that you should unplug the phone and charger.

It takes only a few hours to go from a dead battery to a fully charged battery. Other than the first time you charge the phone, you don't need to wait for the battery to be fully charged. You can partially recharge and run if you want.

In addition to the transformer and USB cable that comes with the phone, you have other optional charging tools:

- **Travel USB charger:** If you already have a USB travel charger, you can leave the transformer at home. This will run you about $15. You still need your cable, although any USB-to-micro USB cable should work.

- **Car charger:** You can buy a charger with a USB port that plugs into the power socket/cigarette lighter in a car. This is convenient if you spend a lot of time in your car. The list price is $30, but you can get the real Samsung car charger for less at some online stores.

- **Photocell or fuel cell charger:** Several companies make products that can charge your phone. Some use photovoltaic cells to transform light into power. As long as there is a USB port (the female part of the USB), all you need is your cable. These can cost from $40 to $100 on up.

Ideally, use Samsung chargers. And if you don't, make sure that any options you use from the preceding list are from a reputable manufacturer. The power specifications for USB ports are standardized. Reputable manufactures comply with these standards, but less reputable manufacturers might not. Cheap USB chargers physically fit the USB end of the cable that goes to your phone. However, Li-ion batteries are sensitive to voltage, and an off-brand USB charger can hurt the performance of your battery.

Li-ion batteries do not like extreme heat. A warm room is one thing, but if you leave your phone on the dashboard all day in Phoenix during the summer, your battery will die. If your phone is with you and you can stand the heat, your battery will be fine.

If you take good care of it, your battery should last about two years, with a drop in performance of about 25 percent from pristine condition out of the box. At that point, you can replace the battery or upgrade to the newest Galaxy S phone.

Navigating the Galaxy S 4

Galaxy S 4 phone devices differ from other phones in that they have significantly fewer hardware buttons (physical buttons on the phone). In their place is a much heavier reliance on software buttons onscreen.

In this section, I guide you through your phone's buttons.

The phone's hardware buttons

Samsung has reduced the number of hardware buttons on the Galaxy S 4 phone device. There are only three: the Power button, the Volume button, and the Home button. Before you get too far, orient yourself to be sure you're looking at the correct side of the phone. The image in Figure 2-6 shows the phone's right side.

Power button

Figure 2-6: The right profile of the Galaxy S 4.

Note: When I refer to the left or right of the phone, I'm assuming a vertical orientation, meaning you're not holding the phone sideways.

The Power button

The Power button is on right side of the phone, when you hold it in vertical orientation, toward the top.

In addition to powering up the phone, pressing the Power button puts the device into sleep mode if you press it for a moment while the phone is on.

Sleep mode shuts off the screen and suspends most running applications.

The phone automatically goes into sleep mode after about 30 seconds of inactivity to save power, but you might want to do this manually when you put away your phone. The Super AMOLED (Active-Matrix Organic Light-Emitting Diode) screen on your Samsung Galaxy S 4 is cool, but it also uses a lot of power.

Don't confuse sleep mode with powering off. Because the screen is the biggest user of power on your phone, having the screen go dark saves battery life. The phone is still alert to any incoming calls; when someone calls, the screen automatically lights up.

The Volume button (s)

Technically, there are two Volume buttons: Volume Up to increase the volume, and Volume Down to lower it. Their location is shown in Figure 2-7.

The Volume buttons control the volume of all the audio sources on the phone, including

- The phone ringer for when a call comes in
- The phone headset when you're talking on the phone
- The volume from the digital music and video player

The Volume controls are aware of the context of what volume you're changing. For example, if you're listening to music, adjusting volume raises or lowers the music volume but leaves the ringer and phone earpiece volumes unchanged.

The Volume buttons are complementary to software settings you can make within the applications. For example, you can open the music player software and turn up the volume on the appropriate screen. Then you can use the hardware buttons to turn down the volume, and you'll see the volume setting on the screen go down.

Volume buttons

Figure 2-7: The Galaxy S 4 Volume buttons on the left.

The Home button

The biggest button the phone is the Home button (see Figure 2-8). It is on the bottom of the front screen.

The Home button brings you back to the home screen from wherever you are in an application. If you are working on applications and feel like you are helplessly lost, don't worry. Press the Home button, close your eyes, tap your heels together three times, and think to yourself, "There's no place like home," and you will be brought back to the Home screen.

You don't really need to do all that other stuff after pressing the Home button. Just pressing the Home button does the trick.

The touchscreen

To cram all the information that you need onto one screen, Samsung takes the modern approach to screen layout. You'll want to become familiar with several finger navigation motions to work with your screen.

Home button

Figure 2-8: The Galaxy S 4 Home button on the front.

Before diving in, though, here's a small list of terms you need to know:

- ✔ **Icon:** This is a little image. Tapping an icon launches an application or performs some function, like making a telephone call.

- ✔ **Button:** A button on a touchscreen is meant to look like a three-dimensional button that you would push on, say, a telephone. Buttons are typically labeled to tell you what it will do when you tap it. For example, you'll see buttons labeled "Save" or "Send."

- ✔ **Hyperlink:** Sometimes called a "link" for short, a hyperlink is text that performs some function when you tap it. Usually, text is lifeless. If you tap a word and it does nothing, it's just text. If you tap a word and it launches a website or causes a screen to pop up, it's a hyperlink.

- ✔ **Thumbnail:** This is a small, low-resolution version of a larger, high-resolution picture stored somewhere else.

With this background, it's time to discuss the motions on the touchscreen you'll be using.

You need to clean the touchscreen glass from time to time. The glass on your phone is Gorilla Glass (made by Corning) and is the toughest stuff available to protect against breakage. Use a soft cloth or microfiber to get off fingerprints. You can even wipe the touchscreen on your clothes. However, never use a paper towel! Over time, glass is no match for fibers in the humble paper towel.

Tap

Often, you just tap the screen to make things happen (like launching an app) or select options. Think of a tap as a single click of a mouse on a computer screen. A tap is simply a touch of the screen, much like using a touchscreen at a retail kiosk. Figure 2-9 shows what the tap motion should look like.

One difference between a mouse click on a computer and a tap on a Galaxy S 4 phone is that a single tap launches applications on the phone in the same way that a double-click of the mouse launches an application on a computer.

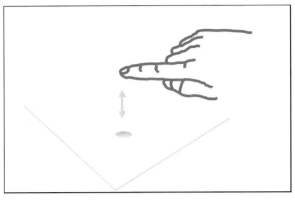

Figure 2-9: The tap motion.

 A tap is different from "press and hold" (see the next section). If you leave your finger on the screen for more than an instant, the phone thinks that you want to do something other than launch an application.

Press and hold

Press and hold, as the name implies, involves putting your finger on an icon on the screen and leaving it there for more than a second. What happens when you leave your finger on an icon depends upon the situation.

For example, when you press and hold on an application on the Home screen (the screen that comes up after you turn on the phone), a garbage can icon appears on the screen. This is to remove that icon from that screen. And when you press and hold an application icon from the list of applications, the phone assumes that you want to copy that application to your Home screen. Don't worry if these distinctions might not make sense yet. The point is that you should be familiar with holding and pressing — and that it's different from tapping.

 You don't need to tap or press and hold very hard for the phone to know that you want it to do something. Neither do you need to worry about breaking the glass, even by pressing on it very hard. If you hold the phone in one hand and tap with the other, you'll be fine. I suppose you might break the glass on the phone if you put it on the floor and press up into a one-fingered handstand. I don't recommend this, but if you do try it, please post the video on YouTube.

On average, a person calls 911 about once every year. Usually, you call 911 because of a stressful situation. The Samsung Galaxy S 4, like every phone, has a special stress sensor that causes it to lock up when you need it most. Okay, not really, but it seems that way. When you are stressed, it's easy to think that you are tapping when you are actually pressing and holding. Be aware of this tendency and remember to tap.

Moving around the screen or to the next screen

Additional finger motions help you move around the screens and to adjust the scaling for images that you want on the screen. Mastering these motions is important to getting the most from your phone.

The first step is navigating the screen to access what's not visible onscreen. Think of this as navigating a regular computer screen, where you use a horizontal scroll bar to access information to the right or left of what's visible on your monitor, or a vertical scroll bar to move you up and down on a screen.

The same concept works on your phone. To overcome the practical realities of screen size on a phone that will fit into your pocket, the Galaxy S 4 phone uses a panorama screen layout, meaning that you keep scrolling left or right (or maybe up and down) to access different screens.

In a nutshell, although the full width of a screen is accessible, only the part bounded by the physical screen of the Galaxy S 4 phone is visible on the display. Depending upon the circumstances, you have several choices on how to get to information not visible on the active screen. These actions include drag, flicks, pinch and stretch, and double taps. I cover all these in the following sections.

Drag

The simplest finger motion on the phone is the drag. You place your finger on a point on the screen and then drag the image with your finger. Then you lift your finger. Figure 2-10 shows what the drag motion looks like.

Figure 2-10: The drag motion for controlled movement.

Dragging allows you to move slowly around the panorama. This motion is like clicking a scroll bar and moving it slowly.

Flick

To move quickly around the panorama, you can flick the screen to move in the direction of your flick (see Figure 2-11).

Better control of this motion comes with practice. In general, the faster the flick, the more the panorama moves. However, some screens, like the extended Home screen, move only one screen to the right or left no matter how fast you flick.

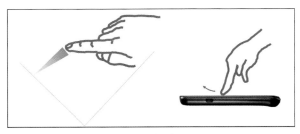

Figure 2-11: Use a flick motion for faster movement.

Pinch and stretch

Some screens allow you to change the scale of images you view on your screen. When this feature is active, the Zoom options change the magnification of the area on the screen. You can zoom out to see more features at a smaller size, or zoom in to see more detail at a larger size.

To zoom out, you put two fingers (apart) on the screen and pull them together to pinch the image. The pinch motion is shown in Figure 2-12.

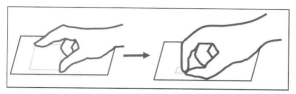

Figure 2-12: Use the pinch motion to zoom out.

The opposite motion is to zoom in. This involves the stretch motion, as shown in Figure 2-13. You place two fingers (close together) and stretch them apart. Make sure you're centered on the spot you want to see in more detail.

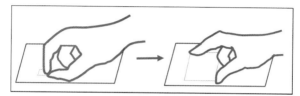

Figure 2-13: Use the stretch motion to zoom in.

Double tap

The double tap (shown in Figure 2-14) just means tapping the same button area on the screen twice in rapid succession. You use the double tap to jump between a zoomed-in and a zoomed-out image to get you back to the previous resolution. This option saves you from any frustration in getting back to a familiar perspective.

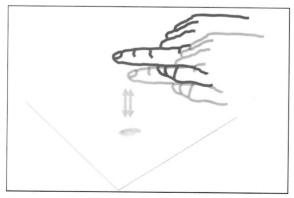

Figure 2-14: The double-tap motion.

Time the taps so that the phone doesn't interpret them as two separate taps. With a little practice, you'll master the timing of the second tap.

The extended Home screen

The extended Home screen (just Home screen, for short) is the first screen that you see when the phone is done setting up. Samsung has set it to be five screen-widths wide and one screen high.

Figure 2-15 shows a representation of the full Home screen layout. At any given moment, of course, you see only one screen at a time.

Figure 2-15: The Galaxy S 4 phone panorama display of the extended Home screen.

The extended Home screen is where you can organize icons and other functions to best make the phone convenient for you. Out of the box, Samsung and your cellular carrier have worked together to create a starting point for you. Beyond that, though, you have lots of ways that you can customize your Home screen so that you have easy access to the things that are most important for you. Much of the book covers all the things that the phone can do, but a recurring theme is how to put those capabilities on your Home screen if you wish.

To start, check out the layout of the Home screen and how it relates to other areas of the phone. Knowing these areas is important for basic navigation.

Figure 2-16 shows a typical Home screen and highlights three important areas on the phone.

✔ **The notification area:** This part of the screen presents you with small icons that let you know if something important is up, like low battery.

✔ **The primary shortcuts:** These five icons remain stationary as you move across the home screen. Samsung and your cellular carrier have determined that these are the four most important applications on your phone.

✔ **The Device Function keys:** These three keys control essential phone functions, regardless of what else is going on at the moment with the phone.

Device Function keys

Primary shortcuts

Notification area

Figure 2-16: Important areas on the Galaxy S 4 phone and Home screen.

There are a series of dots just above the primary shortcuts on the extended home screen. You may also notice that one of the dots isn't just a dot — it is a little house icon. That is the "home" Home screen. The largest dot indicates where you are among the screens. You can navigate among the screens by dragging the screen to the left or right. This moves you one screen at a time. You can also jump multiple screens by tapping on the dot that corresponds to the screen number you want to see, or by dragging the dots to the screen you want to see. Keep reading for more detail on each area.

Adding shortcuts to the Home screen

As seen in Figure 2-15, you have a lot of screen real estate where you can put icons of your favorite applications and widgets (Widgets are small apps that take care of simple functions, like displaying time or the status of your battery). You can add shortcuts to the apps and widgets to your Home screen by following these steps:

1. **From the extended Home screen, tap the Menu button.**

   This brings up a pop-up at the bottom of the screen.

2. **Tap the Add Apps and Widgets button.**

   The screen shown in Figure 2-17 appears. It either displays all the icons of all the apps you currently have on your phone or it shows all the widgets you currently have on your phone. The screen in Figure 2-17 shows the apps. You can see all the apps by sliding around the apps screens.

Figure 2-17: The apps you can add to your Home screen.

If you want to see widgets instead, tap on the word *Widget* towards the top of the screen. It appears slightly grayed out. This takes you to the Widgets screen. Slide your finger across the screen to bring up the different Widgets screens.

3. Press and Hold on the Icon you want.

After you see the app or widget you want to appear on your Home screen, press and hold the icon.

In a few seconds, the app or widget appears on the Home screen you were on most recently. Done.

Taking away shortcuts

Say that you put the shortcut on the wrong screen. No problem. You can press and hold it, and then drag it left or right until it's on the screen you want. Taking a shortcut off your Home screen is simple. Press and hold the shortcut on the screen. In a moment, a garbage can icon appears at the top of the screen. Drag the doomed shortcut to the garbage can, and off it goes to its maker.

It is gone, but if you made a mistake, you can get it back easily enough. To re-create it, simply go back to the App Menu key and follow the process again.

The notification area and screen

As shown in Figure 2-16, the notification area is located at the top of the phone. Here, you see little status icons. Maybe you received a text or an e-mail, or you'll see an application needs some tending to.

Think of the notification area as a special e-mail inbox where your carrier (or even the phone itself) can give you important information about what's happening with your phone. The large icons at the top tell you the condition of the different radio systems on your phone: The number of bars shown gives you an indication of signal strength, and the phone also usually tells you what kind of signal you're getting — like 3G or 4G.

You could take the time to learn the meanings of all the little icons that might come up, but that would take you a while. A more convenient option is to touch the notification area and drag it down, shown in Figure 2-18.

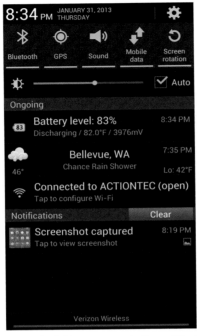

Figure 2-18: Pay attention to the notification screen for important events.

The rest of the screen is written so that you can understand what's going on — and what, if anything, you're expected to do. For example, if you see that you have a new e-mail, you tap the text of the link, and you're taken to your new e-mail.

When you're finished reading the notifications, you slide your finger back up to the top. You can also clear this screen if it gets too full by tapping the Clear button. You can also clear notifications one at a time by touching them and swiping them to the side.

The primary shortcuts

The primary shortcuts are what Samsung and your cellular carrier decided on as the five most important functions of your phone. Each phone type has its own twist on this, but all phones sport a phone icon so that making calls is fast and convenient.

Among the other possible shortcuts here are shortcuts that take you to your contacts, your e-mail, the Internet, texting/messaging, or your list of applications. These shortcuts are not customizable. Don't worry, though. This is not much of a limitation.

The Device Function keys

At the bottom of the screen, below the rectangular screen displays, are three important buttons, the Device Function keys. They're always present for you to navigate your phone even though the backlight might switch off to hide their presence. Whatever else you're doing on the phone, these buttons can take over.

The button on the left of the Home button is the Menu key. Tapping it brings up a list of options you can select. The key to the right of the Home button is a Return key. If it is lit, you can tap it and it will take you back one step.

 The Device Function keys are kind of cool because they light up when you are touching them or the screen, and fade away the rest of the time.

The Menu button

Tapping the Menu button brings up a pop-up menu at the bottom of the screen from which you can access valuable capabilities. What's "valuable" depends upon what application is running at that time.

The Home button

As I discussed earlier, pressing the Home button takes you directly to the extended Home screen.

 The Home button comes in handy when you want to change what you're doing with the phone, such as going from browsing the web to making a phone call.

The Back button

The Back button on your phone is similar to the Back button in a web browser: It takes you back one screen.

As you start navigating through the screens on your phone, pressing the Back button takes you back to the previous screen. If you keep pressing the Back button, you'll eventually return to the Home screen.

The keyboard

The screen of the Galaxy S 4 phone is important, but you'll still probably spend more time entering data on the QWERTY keyboard.

Using the software keyboard

The software keyboard automatically pops up when the application detects a need for user text input. The keyboard appears at the bottom of the screen.

For example, say you're in Seattle, searching for the Seattle Art Museum via the Mapping application. Tap the Search button, and the keyboard pops up onscreen, as shown in Figure 2-19.

In this case, a text box pops up in addition to the keyboard. As you type **Seattle Art Museum**, the text appears in the box on the screen as if you had typed it on a hardware keyboard. The phone is smart enough to know when the keyboard should appear and disappear. If the keyboard doesn't appear when you want to start typing, you can tap on the text box where you want to enter data.

Using Swype

Galaxy S 4 phones come with an enhanced data-entering capability called Swype. This option automatically comes with your phone, and with a little practice, can dramatically speed your ability to type fast on your phone.

Here's how Swype works: Instead of tapping each discrete key on the keyboard, you leave your finger on the screen and swipe from key to key. The Swype application figures out the words you are wanting to type, including inserting the spaces automatically.

If you like Swype, you can use it any time that you're entering data. If you don't care for it, you can just tap your letters. It's all up to you!

When you are done, you can tap the "done" button, or just be quiet. Within a few seconds, you will see what you said!

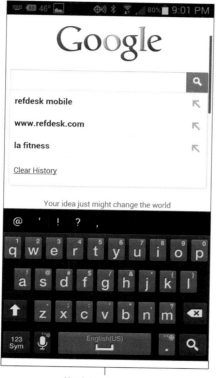

Keyboard pop-up

Figure 2-19: Use the software keyboard to enter data.

The orientation of the phone

In the earlier section where I discuss the Power button, I referred to the phone being in vertical orientation (so that the phone is tall and narrow). It can also be used in the landscape orientation (sideways, or so that the phone is short and wide). The phone senses which direction you're holding it and orients the screen to make it easier for you to view.

The phone makes its orientation known to the application, but not all applications are designed to change their inherent display. That nuance is left to the writers of the application. For example, your phone can play videos. However, the video player application that comes with your phone shows video in landscape mode only.

In addition, the phone can sense when you are holding it to your ear. When it senses that it is held in this position, it shuts off the screen. You need not be concerned that you will accidentally "chin dial" a number in Botswana.

Going to Sleep Mode/ Turning Off the Phone

You can leave your phone on every minute until you're ready to upgrade to the newest Galaxy S 4 phone in a few years, but that will use up your battery in no time. Instead, put your idle phone in sleep mode to save battery power. *Note:* This also happens automatically after 30 seconds of inactivity on the screen.

 You can adjust the screen timeout for a longer duration, or you can manually put the phone in sleep mode by pressing the Power button for just a moment.

Sometimes it's best to simply shut down the phone if you aren't going to use it for several days or more. To shut down the phone completely, simply press and hold the Power button for a few seconds. The following options appear:

- **Silent mode:** Turn off sound.

- **Airplane mode:** Turns off the radios that communicate to the local Wi-Fi access point and the cellular network so that you can't receive or make voice calls or send or receive texts or data. As the name implies, use this setting when you're flying, but you want to use applications that can operate without a data connection, such as some games or e-mail. Because some flights now provide Wi-Fi, the phone *does* allow you to turn Wi-Fi back on when you're in airplane mode if you need it.

- **Power Off:** Shut down the phone completely.

Good night!

3

Calling People

*A*t its essence, any cellphone — no matter how fancy or smart — exists to make phone calls. The good news is that making and receiving phone calls on your Galaxy S 4 is easy.

In this chapter, I show you how not only how to make a call but how to use your call list to keep track of your calls. And don't skip the section on using your phone for emergencies.

Finally, if you're like many people, you're never doing just one thing at a time, and a Bluetooth headset can make it easier for you to talk on the phone while driving, wrangling kids and dogs, or just plain living life. In this chapter, I show you how to hook up your phone to a Bluetooth headset so you can make and receive phone calls hands-free.

Making Calls

After your phone is on and you're connected to your cellular carrier (see Chapters 1 and 2), you can make a phone call. It all starts from the Home screen. Along the bottom of the screen, above the Device Function keys, are five icons, which are the *primary shortcuts* (see Figure 3-1). *Note:* From left to right, they are

    ✓ Phone

    ✓ Contacts

✔ Messaging

✔ Internet

✔ Apps

Primary shortcuts

Figure 3-1: The primary shortcuts on the Home screen.

To make a call, follow these steps:

1. **From the Home screen, tap the Phone icon.**

   The Keypad screen (see Figure 3-2) appears. This looks like a stylized version of a touch pad on a regular landline phone.

2. **Tap the telephone number you want to call.**

   Don't be alarmed if you don't hear a dial tone until you tap Send; smartphones don't connect to a network and start a dial tone until after you dial your number.

Figure 3-2: Dial the number from the Keypad screen.

For long distance calls while in the U.S., you don't need to dial 1 before the area code — just dial the area code and then the seven-digit phone number. Similarly, you can omit the "1" and the area code for local calls. On the other hand, if you are traveling internationally, you need to include the "1" and be prepared for international roaming charges!

In Chapter 6, you can read about how to make a phone call through your contacts.

3. **Tap the green Send button at the bottom of the screen to place the call.**

Within a few seconds, you should hear the phone ringing at the other end or a busy signal.

4. **When you're done with your call, tap the End button — the red button at the bottom of the screen.**

The call is disconnected.

If the call doesn't go through, either the cellular coverage where you are is insufficient, or your phone got switched to Airplane mode. It is possible that your cellular carrier let you out of the door without having set you up for service, but that's pretty unlikely!

Check the notification section of your phone at the top of the screen. If there are no connection strength bars, try moving to another location. If you see a small plane silhouette, bring down the notification screen (see how in Chapter 2) and tap the plane icon to turn off Airplane mode.

If you pull down the notification screen and do not see the green silhouette of an airplane, scroll the green or gray icons to the left. This icon may be off the page. Alternatively, tap the icon with the boxes in the upper-right corner and you will see all the notification icons, as shown in Figure 3-3.

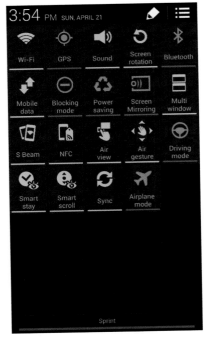

Figure 3-3: The notification icons.

Answering Calls

Receiving a call is even easier than making a call. When someone calls you, caller ID information appears along with three icons. Figure 3-4 shows a typical screen for an incoming call.

Uriah Heap
425-555-1212

Incoming call

Reject call with message

Figure 3-4: The screen when you're receiving a call.

To answer the call, put your finger on the green phone icon and slide it to the right. To not answer a call, you can simply ignore the ringing or you can put your finger on the red phone icon and slide it to the left. The ringing stops immediately. In either case, the call will go to voicemail.

Regardless of what you were doing on the phone at that moment — such as listening to music or playing a game — the answer screen can appear. Any active application, including music or video, is suspended until the call is over.

You must set up your voicemail for callers to leave you messages. If you haven't yet set up your voicemail, the caller will hear a recorded message saying that your voicemail account isn't yet set up. Some cellular carriers can set up voicemail for you when you activate the account and get the phone; others require you to set up voicemail on your own. Ask how voicemail works at your carrier store or look for instructions in the manual included with your phone.

Keeping Track of Your Calls: The Call List

One of the nice features of cellular phones is that the phone keeps a record of the calls that you've made and received. Sure, you might have caller ID on your landline at home or work, but most landline phones don't keep track of who you called. Cellphones, on the other hand, keep track of all the numbers you've called. This information can be very convenient, like when you want to return a call, and you don't have that number handy. In addition, you can easily add a number to the contact list on your phone.

By tapping the "Recent" icon, you get a list of all incoming and outgoing calls. (This icon, located at the top of the screen, is a phone receiver with arrows pointing to it and away; see Figure 3-2.) Each call bears an icon telling you whether it was an

- **Outgoing call you made:** An orange arrow points to the number.

- **Incoming call you received:** A green arrow points away from the number.

- **Incoming call you missed:** A red phone silhouette with a broken arrow.

- **Incoming call you ignored:** A blue slash sign is next to the phone icon.

A typical call log is shown in Figure 3-5.

By tapping any number in your call list, you see a screen like the one shown in Figure 3-6. From this screen, you can do several things:

- See the date and time the call was logged and all previous calls to and from this number.

- Call the number by tapping the green call button.

- Send a text to that number by tapping the number and then tapping Send Message on the pop-up screen that appears. (More on this in Chapter 4.)

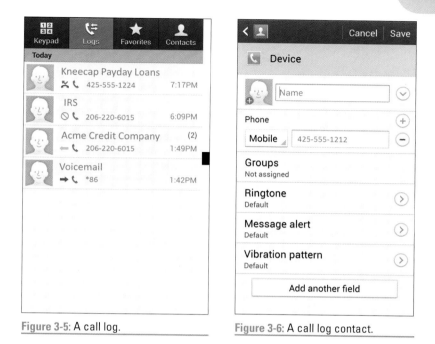

Figure 3-5: A call log.

Figure 3-6: A call log contact.

- Mark that number as a favorite by tapping the star icon. Your favorites appear on the Keypad screen (refer to Figure 3-2), which saves you from having to dial those numbers.

- Add the number to your contacts list by tapping the "Create Contact" button. A pop-up gives you the option to add it to you contacts, either by creating a new contact or adding to an existing one. I cover contacts more in Chapter 6.

Making an Emergency Call: The 411 on 911

Cellphones are wonderful tools for calling for help in an emergency. The Samsung Galaxy S 4, like all phones in the United States and Canada, can make emergency calls to 911.

Just tap the Phone icon on the Home screen, tap **911**, and then tap Send. You'll be routed to the 911 call center nearest to your location. This works wherever you are within the United States. So, say you live in Chicago but have a car accident in Charlotte; just tap 911 to be connected to the 911 call center in Charlotte, not Chicago.

Even if your phone isn't registered on a network, you don't have a problem. You phone lets you know that the only number you can dial is a 911 call center.

Syncing a Bluetooth Headset

With a Bluetooth headset device, you can talk on your phone without needing to hold the phone and without any cords running from the phone to your earpiece. You've probably come across plenty of people talking on Bluetooth headsets. You might even have wondered whether they were a little crazy, talking to themselves. Well, call yourself crazy now, because when you start using a Bluetooth headset, you might never want to go back.

Not surprisingly, Galaxy S 4 phones can connect to Bluetooth devices. The first step to using a Bluetooth headset with your phone is to sync the two devices. Here's how:

1. **From the Home screen on your phone, tap the Apps icon.**

   This gets you to the list of all the applications on your phone.

2. **Flick or pan to the Settings icon and tap it.**

   The Settings icon is shown here. This screen holds most of the settings that you can adjust on your phone.

   Tapping on the Settings icon brings up the screen seen in Figure 3-7.

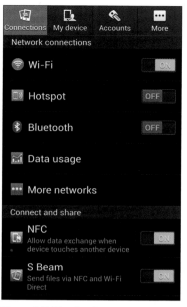

Figure 3-7: The Settings screen.

3. Tap the Bluetooth Off button to toggle it to On.

Be careful not to tap the green button to the right of the Bluetooth icon and title if it is set to On. This would turn off Bluetooth. That defeats the purpose.

4. Tap the Bluetooth icon.

This brings up Figure 3-8.

5. Tap the box to the right of the title of your Phone's model number.

This enables your phone to be visible to other Bluetooth devices. This state will last for 120 seconds. That is enough time for you to get your Bluetooth devices into pairing mode so they can negotiate the proper security settings and pair up every time they "see" each other going forward.

6. Tap the bar at the bottom with the word *Scan*.

Your phone scans the area for other Bluetooth devices.

Bluetooth screen   Bluetooth screen in pairing mode

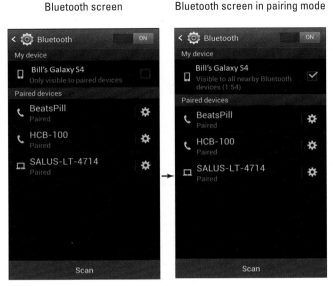

Figure 3-8: The Bluetooth Settings screen.

7. Put your headset into syncing mode.

Follow the instructions that came with your headset.

After a moment, the phone "sees" the headset. When it does, you are prompted to enter the security code, and the software keyboard pops up.

8. Enter the security code for your headset and then tap the Enter button.

The security code on most headsets is 0000, but check the instructions that came with your headset if that number doesn't work.

Your phone might see other devices in the immediate area. If so, it asks you which device you want to pair with. Tap the name of your headset.

Your headset is now synced to your phone. If you turn one on when the other is already on, they recognize each other and automatically pair up.

4

The Joy of Text

*S*ure, cellphones are made for talking. But these days, many people use their cellphones even more for texting. *Text messages* (short messages, usually 160 characters or less, sent by cellphone) are particularly convenient when you can't talk at the moment (maybe you're in a meeting or class) or when you just have a small bit of information to share ("Running late — see you soon!").

Many cellphone users — particularly younger ones — prefer sending texts to making a phone call. They find texting a faster and more convenient way to communicate, and they often use texting shorthand to fit more "content" in that character limit.

Even the most basic phones support texting these days, but your Galaxy S 4 phone makes sending and receiving text messages more convenient, no matter whether you're an occasional or pathological texter. In this chapter, I fill you in on how to send a text message (with or without an attachment), how to receive a text message, and how to read your old text messages.

To use text messaging, you must have texting capability as part of your service plan. See Chapter 1 for more info.

Sending the First Text Message

There are two scenarios for texting. The first is when you send someone a text for the first time. The second is when you have a text conversation with a person.

When you first get your phone and are ready to brag about your new Galaxy S 4 and want to send a text to your best friend, here's how easy it is:

1. On the Home screen, tap the Messaging icon.

The Messaging application is between the contacts and the Internet icons. When you tap it, you will get a mostly blank home texting screen. This is shown in Figure 4-1.

Figure 4-1: The Messaging Home screen.

When you have some conversations going, it begins to fill up. More on that soon.

2. **Tap the New Message icon (the pencil hovering over a blank page).**

Tapping the New Message icon brings up the screen seen in Figure 4-2.

Figure 4-2: A blank texting screen.

3. **Tap to enter the ten-digit mobile telephone number of the recipient.**

A text box appears at the top of the screen with the familiar To field at the top. The keyboard appears at the bottom of the screen.

As shown in Figure 4-3, the top field is where you type in the telephone number. The numerals are along the top of the keyboard.

Be sure to include the area code, even if the person you are texting is local. However, there is no need to put a "1" before the number.

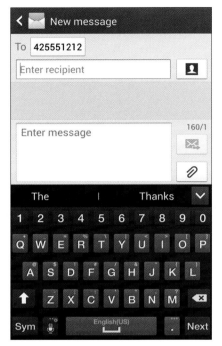

Figure 4-3: Type the recipient's number in the upper text box.

If this is your first text, you haven't had a chance to build up a history of texts. After you've been using your messaging application for a while, you will have already entered contact information.

4. **To write your text message, tap the text box that says Enter Message. Figure 4-4 shows you where to enter your text.**

Your text message can be up to 160 characters, including spaces and punctuation. The application counts down the number of characters you have left.

5. **Send the text by tapping the Send button to the right of your message.**

The Send button is the one with the image of an envelope with the arrow on it. The phone takes it from here. Within a few seconds, the message is sent to your friend's cellphone.

Type your message here.

Recipient's number

Figure 4-4: Type your text here.

 After you build your contact list (read about this in Chapter 6), you can tap a name from the contact list or start typing a name in the recipient text box. If there's only one number for that contact, your phone assumes that's the receiving phone you want to send a text to. If that contact has multiple numbers, it asks you which phone number you want to send your text to.

 You've probably heard a thousand times about how it is a very bad idea to text while you are driving. Here comes one thousand and one. It is a *very bad idea* to text while you are driving — and illegal in some places. There are Dummies who read this book (and are actually very smart), and then there are DUMMIES who text and drive. Be the former and not the latter.

Carrying on a Conversation via Texting

In the bad ol' pre-Galaxy S days, most cellular phones would keep a log of your texts. The phone would keep each text that you sent or received in sequential order, regardless of who sent or received them.

Texts stored sequentially are old-school. Your Galaxy S 4 keeps track of the contact with which you have been texting and puts it into a "conversation."

In Figure 4-5, you can see that the first page for messaging refers to *conversations*. After you start texting someone, those texts are stored in one conversation.

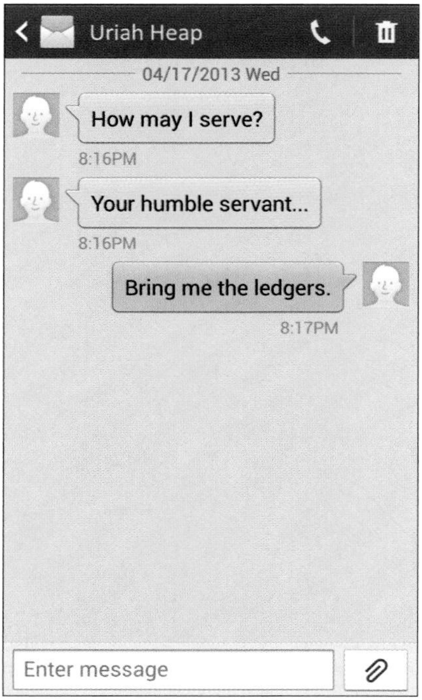

Figure 4-5: A messaging conversation.

As Figure 4-5 shows, each text message is presented in sequence, with the author of the text indicated by the direction of the text balloon.

Note the Type to Compose text box at the bottom of the screen. With this convenient feature, you can send whatever you type to the person with whom you're having a conversation.

In the bad old days, it was sometimes hard to keep straight the different texting conversations you were having. When you start a texting conversation with someone else, there is a second conversation.

Before too long, you will have multiple conversations going on. Don't worry. You don't need to keep the conversation going all the time. No one thinks twice if you do not text for a while. The image in Figure 4-6 shows how the text page from Figure 4-1 can look before too long.

Figure 4-6: The Text screen showing multiple conversations.

Sending an Attachment with a Text

What if you want to send something in addition to or instead of text? Say, you want to send a picture, some music, or a Word document along with your text. Easy as pie, as long as the phone on the receiving end can recognize the attachment. Here is the recipe:

1. **From the Home screen, tap the Messaging icon.**

2. **Either tap the New Message icon and enter the number of the intended recipient, or pick up on an existing conversion.**

   You'll see the text creation page from Figure 4-3. Enter the information you want like a normal text.

3. **To add an attachment, tap the icon that looks like a paper clip.**

   The paper clip icon brings up the screen you see in Figure 4-7.

4. **Tap your file type choice, and your phone presents you with the options that fall into that category.**

   This asks what kind of file you want to attach. Your choices include pictures, videos, audio files, and some others I will describe later. For now, it's just good that you know that you have options.

   After you select the file, it becomes an attachment to your text message.

5. **Continue typing your text message, if needed.**

6. **When you're done with the text portion of the message, tap the Send Text button, and off it all goes.**

A simple text message is an SMS (short message service) message. When you add an attachment, you're sending an MMS (multimedia messaging service) message. Back in the day, MMS messages cost more to send and receive than SMS messages did. These days, that isn't the case in the United States.

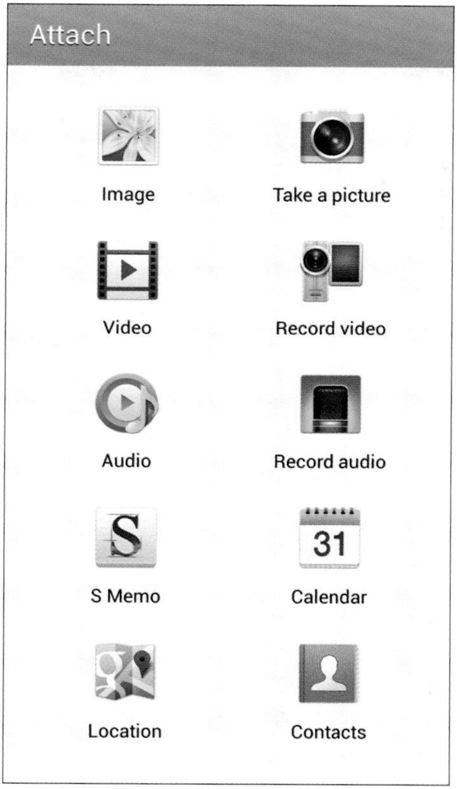

Figure 4-7: Tap the Attach button to attach a file to a text.

Receiving Text Messages

Receiving a text is even easier than sending one.

When you're having a text conversation and you receive a new text from the person you're texting with, your phone signals that you have a message. It beeps, or vibrates if you have the sound off. Also, the notification area of the screen (the very top) indicates that you have a text by showing a very small version of the messaging icon.

You can either pull down the notification screen from the very top of the screen or start the messaging application. Your choice.

If an attachment comes along, it's included in the conversation screens.

To access the text, you need to unlock the screen. The Messaging icon, an envelope, also displays the number of new texts that you have. Tap that icon to open the conversations.

Managing Your Text History

The Messaging Conversations screen stores and organizes all your texts until you delete them. You should clean up this screen every now and then.

The simplest option for managing your messages is to tap the Menu icon and then tap Delete Threads. You can then select and unselect all the conversations that you want deleted. Tap the Delete link at the bottom of the screen, and they disappear.

 Practice good texting hygiene. Regularly clear out older texts. It's highly unlikely that you need to keep 200 texts from anyone. Starting a new conversation is easy enough, anyway.

Another deletion option is to open the conversation. You can delete each text by pressing and holding on the balloon. After a moment, a menu appears from which you can delete that message. This method is a lot slower if you have lots of texts, though.

5

Sending and Receiving E-Mail

*I*f you've had e-mail on your phone for a while, you know how convenient it is. If your Galaxy S 4 phone is your first cellphone with the capability to send and receive e-mail, prepare to be hooked.

I start this chapter by showing you how to set up your e-mail, regardless of whether your e-mail is supported (more on that in a bit). Then I show you how to read and manage your e-mails. Finally, I tell you how to write and send e-mails.

Your phone primarily interacts with your inbox on your e-mail account. It isn't really set up to work like the full-featured e-mail application on your computer, though. For example, many e-mail packages integrate with a sophisticated word processor, have sophisticated filing systems for your saved messages, and offer an extensive selection of fonts. As long as you do not mind working without these advanced capabilities, you might never need to get on your computer to access your e-mail again, and you could store e-mails in folders on your phone. However, the phone access to e-mail is best used in working with the e-mails that are in your inbox.

Using e-mail on your phone requires a data connection. Some cellular carriers solve this problem by obliging you to have a data plan with your phone. If your cellular carrier does not, you won't be able to use e-mail unless you're connected to a Wi-Fi hotspot. I recommend that you get that data plan and enjoy the benefits of wireless e-mail.

Setting Up Your E-Mail

Your phone can manage up to ten e-mail accounts from the Email app on your phone. With a Galaxy S 4 phone (unlike some other phones), you may need to create a separate e-mail account just for your phone. However, you will miss out on so many exciting capabilities that I highly recommend setting up a new Gmail account if you don't have one already (more on that later). You need a Gmail account to access the Google Play Store that you use to download new applications for your phone. A Gmail account is also the means to back up your contacts and calendar and it offers access to sharing photos. Without a Gmail account, you miss out on many of the best features on the Galaxy S 4.

The Email app on your phone routinely polls all the e-mail systems for which you give an e-mail account and password. It then presents you with a copy of your e-mails.

Setup is so easy and makes you so productive that I advise you to consider adding all your e-mail accounts to your phone.

Getting ready

In general, connecting to a personal e-mail account simply involves entering the name of your e-mail account and its password in your phone. Have these handy when you are ready to set up your phone.

These days, many of us have multiple personal e-mail address for many reasons. Just have the e-mail account and password ready, and you can add all of them. You do need to pick one account as your favorite. Although you can send an e-mail using any of the accounts, your phone wants to know the e-mail account that you want it to use as a default.

The advantages of getting a Gmail account

You might already have a work and a personal e-mail account. You might even have an old e-mail account that you check only once in a while because some friends, for whatever reason, haven't updated their profile for you and continue to use an old address.

The thought of getting yet another e-mail address, even one that's free, might (understandably) be unappealing. After all, it's another address and password to remember. However, some important functions on your phone require that you have a Gmail account. These include

✓ The ability to buy applications from the Play Store. (This is huge!) I go over the Play Store in Chapter 8.

✓ Free access to the photo site Picasa (although other sites have many of the same features). I cover Picasa and photo options in Chapter 9.

✓ Access to the Music and Video Hub.

✓ Automatic backup of your contacts and calendar. That's explained in more detail in Chapter 6.

To make a long story short, it's worth the trouble to get a Gmail account, even if you already have a personal e-mail account.

Next, you may want to have access to your work account. This is relatively common these days, but some companies see this as a security problem. You should consult with your IT department for some extra information. Technologically, it is not hard to make this kind of thing happen as long as your business e-mail is reasonably modern.

Finally, if you do not already have a Gmail account, I strongly encourage you to get one. Read the nearby sidebar, "The advantages of getting a Gmail account" to find out why.

Setting up your existing Gmail account

If you already have a Gmail account, setup is easy as can be. Follow these steps from the Apps menu:

1. **Find the Gmail icon in the Apps list.**

   Here is the most confusing part. The icon on the left in Figure 5-1 is the Gmail app. The icon on the right is the icon for all your other e-mail accounts.

Figure 5-1: The Mail icons in the Apps list. _____

2. **Tap the Gmail icon.**

   Because your phone does not know if you have a Gmail account, it asks you whether this is a new account, as shown in Figure 5-2.

Add a Google Account

Do you want to add an existing account or create a new one?

Existing

New

Figure 5-2: Is this a new or existing account? _____

3. **Tap the Existing button on the screen.**

   This brings up the screen in Figure 5-3.

Figure 5-3: The Gmail sign-in screen.

4. Enter your existing Gmail user ID and password.

Go ahead and type your e-mail account address and your password. When you are ready, tap Done on the keyboard.

You may get a pop-up re-confirming that you agree with the terms of use and all that legal stuff. Tap OK. You'll see lots of flashing lights and whirling circles while your phone and your Gmail account get to know each other.

If everything is correct, your phone and your account get acquainted and become best friends. After a few minutes, they are ready to serve your needs. If you have a problem, you probably mistyped something. Try retyping your information in again.

From this point on, any e-mail you get on your Gmail account will also appear on your phone!

Setting up a new Gmail account

If you need to set up a new Gmail account, you have a few more steps to follow. Before I get into the steps, think up a good user ID and password.

Gmail has been around for a while. That means all the good, simple e-mail addresses are taken. Unless you plan to start using this e-mail account as your primary e-mail, which you could do if you wanted, you are probably best off if you pick some unusual combination of letters and numbers that you can remember for now to get through this process.

When you have this ready, follow Steps 1 and 2 in the previous section, but tap New instead of Existing when you get to the screen in Figure 5-2. From there, follow these steps:

1. **Enter your first and last names on the screen.**

   Google asks you for your name in the screen shown in Figure 5-4. This is how they personalize any communications they have with you. Enter them and tap Next on the keypad.

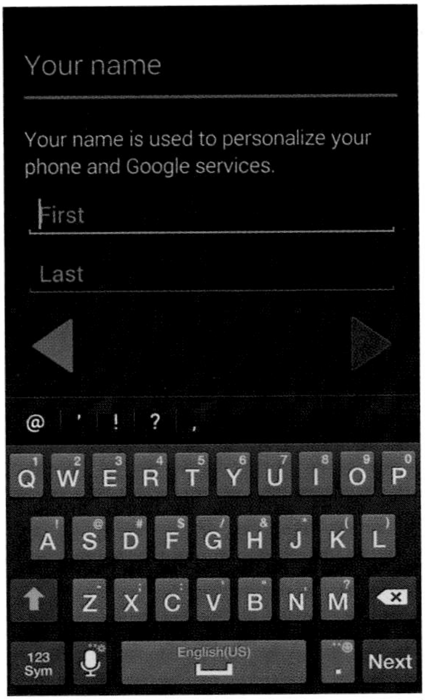

Figure 5-4: Enter your first and last name on this screen.

2. Enter the username you want to use with Gmail and tap Done.

On the screen shown in Figure 5-5, enter the username you want. Hopefully you get this name on the first shot.

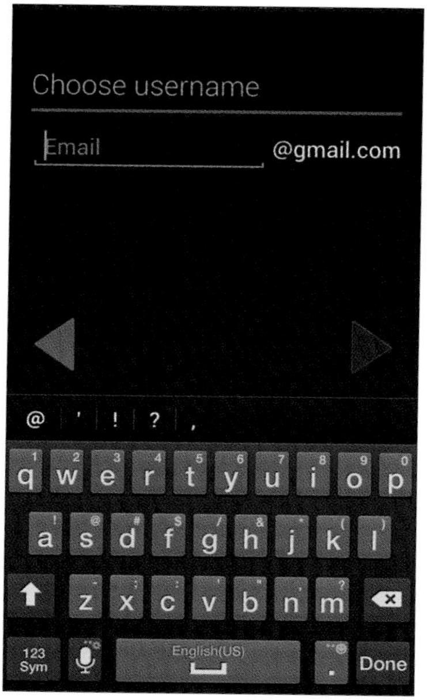

Figure 5-5: The Username screen.

If your first choice isn't available, try again. There is no easy way to check before you do these steps. Eventually, you hit on an unused ID. When you are successful, it will congratulate you.

3. Accept the terms and conditions of the account.

You may want a lawyer to review this. Or not. Basically, the terms are that you should be nice and not try to cheat anyone. Don't abuse the privilege of having the account.

4. Verify the funny-looking writing.

Google wants to make sure that you are a real person and not a computer program out to clog up a valid user ID. You will see a screen that looks like Figure 5-6.

Figure 5-6: The Authenticating screen.

5. **Prepare a security question and an alternate e-mail address.**

   If you forget your password, Google wants to verify that you are really you and not someone pretending to be you. They do this by asking you a security question and then asking for another e-mail account where they can send your temporary password. These screens show you where to enter your information and the question choices.

6. **Join Google+ if you want.**

   The next screen asks if you want to join Google+. You can if you want, but I suggest that you come back to it another time. The sooner you get your Gmail account set up, the more fun you can have. Tap Done.

After you tap Done, light flashes and you see the screen shown in Figure 5-7.

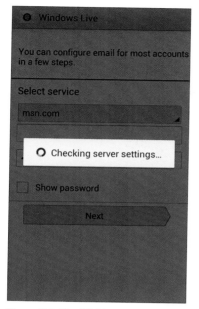

Figure 5-7: The Waiting screen.

It usually takes less than five minutes. While you wait, you'll see all kinds of messages that it is getting ready to sync things. Don't worry. I'll explain these messages in good time. For now, you can add any other e-mail accounts you want by following the steps in the next section.

Working with non-Gmail e-mail accounts

Your phone is set up to work with up to ten e-mail accounts. If you have more than ten accounts, I'm thinking that you might have too much going on in your life. No phone, not even the Galaxy S 4, can help you there!

To set up an e-mail account other than Gmail to work with your phone, go to the Home screen. Look for the simple Mail icon; it has an envelope icon on it (see Figure 5-1). This is probably on your Home screen as one of the five primary shortcuts just above the Device Function keys or in your application list.

After you tell your phone all your emails, the first Email screen will have all your e-mails from all your e-mail accounts. This allows you to look at all the messages. In addition, each account has its own inbox. You can choose which option works best for you.

1. **Tap the Menu icon from the Email screen.**

   This brings up a menu that looks like the image shown in Figure 5-8.

2. **Tap the Others icon.**

   This is a generic way to enter lots of kinds of e-mail accounts. Tapping it brings up a screen that looks like the image shown in Figure 5-9.

Figure 5-8: The menu for the Email app.   Figure 5-9: The Set Up Email screen.

3. **Carefully enter your full e-mail account name, and then enter your password in the second field.**

   Your e-mail address should include the full shebang, including the @ sign and everything that follows it. Make sure to enter your password correctly, being careful with capitalization if your e-mail server is case-sensitive — most are. If in doubt, select the option to let you see your password.

4. **Decide whether you want this account to be your default e-mail account.**

   After you add multiple accounts to your phone, only one account can be your primary, or default, account. Although you can send an e-mail from any of the accounts registered on your phone, you have to select one as the default. If you want this account to be the primary or default account, select the Send Email from This Account by Default check box. If not, leave that option as it is.

5. **Tap Next.**

   You see all kinds of options you can select. Just go with the default settings for now.

6. **Tap OK.**

   If everything goes as planned, your phone and your e-mail account will start chatting.

7. **Enter names for the new e-mail account.**

   You can always use the e-mail address for the name, but I recommend choosing something shorter, like Joe's MSN or My Hotmail.

8. **Tap Done.**

Don't forget to check that everything has gone as planned and is set up to your liking. Go back to the Home screen, tap the Email icon, open Settings, and tap the + (plus) sign to add new accounts.

Using Figure 5-10 as an example, you can see that my account is now registered on my phone. It worked!

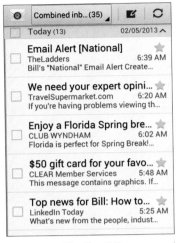

Figure 5-10: The Email Home screen.

Setting up a corporate e-mail account

In addition to personal e-mail accounts, you can add your work e-mail to your phone — if it's based upon a Microsoft Exchange server, that is, and if it's okay with your company's IT department.

Before you get started, you need some information from the IT department of your company:

- The domain name of the office e-mail server
- Your work e-mail password
- The name of your exchange server

If the folks in IT are okay with you using your phone to access its e-mail service, your IT department will have no trouble supplying you with this information.

Before you set up your work e-mail on your phone, make sure that you have permission. If you do this without the green light from your company, and you end up violating your company's rules, you could be in hot water. Increasing your productivity won't be much help if you're standing out in the parking lot holding all the contents of your office in a cardboard box.

Assuming that your company wants you to be more productive with no extra cost to the company, the process for adding your work e-mail starts at your e-mail Home screen seen in Figure 5-8. In fact, all the steps are the same as the previous section up to Step 4, so use those steps and then come back here in place of Step 5.

1. **Tap Manual Setup.**

2. **Tap Exchange Account.**

   This brings up a screen like that shown in Figure 5-11. Some of the fields might be populated based upon the information that you entered at Step 5 in the preceding step list.

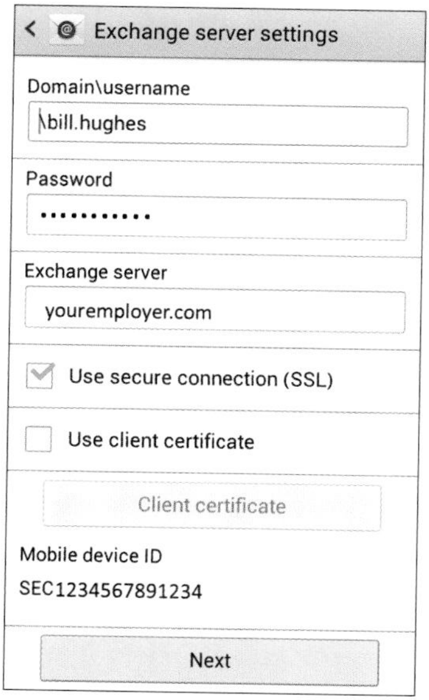

Figure 5-11: The Manual Setup screen for adding corporate e-mail accounts.

3. **Verify that information and enter any missing data according to what your IT department provided you.**

4. **Tap Next.**

   This begins syncing with your work e-mail.

   Within a minute, you should start seeing your work e-mail messages appearing. If this doesn't happen, contact the IT department at your employer.

Reading E-Mail on Your Phone

In Figure 5-11, you can see how the e-mail screen looks for e-mail when you have multiple e-mail accounts. This screen is set up so that it combines all your e-mails into one inbox. At any given time, you might want to look at the accounts individually or all together.

To look at all your e-mails in one large inbox, tap Combined Inbox. This lists all your e-mails in chronological order. To open any e-mail, just tap it.

If, on the other hand, you want to see just e-mails from one account, tap the box at the top that says Combined Inbox. When you tap it, it displays a drop-down menu with all the individual e-mail accounts. Tap on the account you want to focus on at the moment, and your phone will bring up your e-mails in chronological order for just that e-mail address.

Writing and Sending an E-Mail

After you set up the receiving part of e-mail, the other important side is composing and sending e-mails. At any time when you're in an e-mail screen, simply tap the Menu button to get a pop-up screen. There, tap the Compose icon.

Here's the logic as to which e-mail account will be assigned to ultimately send this e-mail:

  ✔ If you're in the inbox of an e-mail account and you tap the Compose icon after tapping Menu, your phone sends the e-mail to the intended recipient(s) through that account.

  ✔ If you're in the combined inbox or some other part of the e-mail application, your phone assumes that you want to send the e-mail from the default e-mail account that you selected when you registered your second (or additional) e-mail account.

When you tap the Compose icon in the Menu pop-up menu, it tells you which account it will use. The Email composition screen in Figure 5-12 shows this e-mail will be coming from this account: galaxysfordummies@gmail.com.

As shown in this screen, the top has a stalwart To field, where you type the address of the intended recipient. You can also call up your contacts, a group, or your most recent e-mail addresses. (Read all about contacts in Chapter 6.) You tap the address or contact you want, and it populates the To field.

Figure 5-12: The Email composition screen.

Below that, in the Subject field, is where you enter the subject of the e-mail. And below that is the body of the e-mail, with the default signature, Sent from my Samsung Galaxy S 4, although this signature might have been customized for your cellular carrier.

At the top of the screen are two icons:

  ✓ **Send:** Tap this icon, which looks like an envelope with an arrow, to send the e-mail to the intended recipient(s).

  ✓ **Attach:** Tap this paperclip icon to attach a file of any variety to your e-mail.

If you change your mind about sending an e-mail, you can just tap the Back key. If you're partially done with the message, you're asked whether you want to save it in your Drafts folder.

The Drafts folder, seen in Figure 5-13, works like the Drafts folder in your computer's e-mail program. When you want to continue working on a saved e-mail, you open the Drafts folder, tap on it, and continue working.

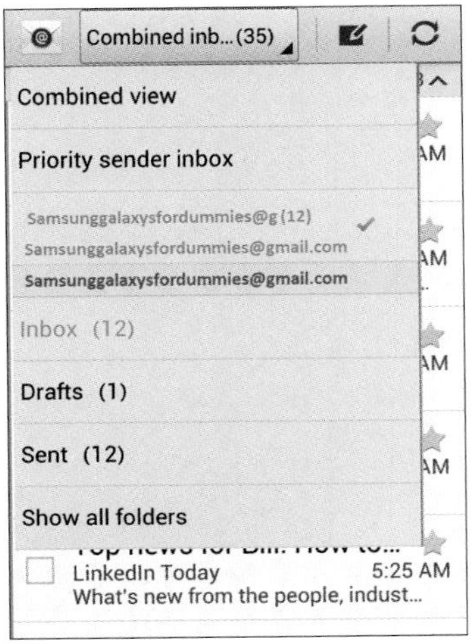

| ⊚ | Combined inb...(35) ◢ | ✉ | ↻ |

Combined view

Priority sender inbox

Samsunggalaxysfordummies@g (12)
Samsunggalaxysfordummies@gmail.com
Samsunggalaxysfordummies@gmail.com

Inbox (12)

Drafts (1)

Sent (12)

Show all folders

☐ LinkedIn Today   5:25 AM
What's new from the people, indust...

Figure 5-13: Email folders stored on your phone.

Replying to and Forwarding E-mails

Replying to or forwarding the e-mails that you get is a common activity. You can do this from your Email app.

You can Reply by tapping the button with the return arrow visible at the top of the screen. If other people were copied on the email, there will be a single return arrow to Reply to just the sender and a double return arrow you can tap to Reply All.

When you tap either of these options, the Reply screen comes back with the To line populated by the sender's e-mail address (or addresses) and a blank space where you can leave your comments.

To forward the e-mail, tap the appropriate Menu option of the Device Function keys. After you tap Forward, you enter the addressee just like you do when sending a new e-mail.

6

Entering Your Contacts

In This Chapter

▶ Putting all your callers, texters, and e-mailers on your phone

▶ Getting all your contacts in one location

*Y*ou're probably familiar with using contact databases. Many cellphones automatically create one, or at least prompt you to create one. You also probably have a file of contacts on your work computer, comprising work e-mail addresses and telephone numbers. And if you have a personal e-mail account, you probably have a contact database of e-mail accounts of friends and family members. If you're kickin' it old school, you might even keep a paper address book with names, addresses, and telephone numbers.

The problem with having all these contact databases is that it's rarely ever as neat and tidy as I've just outlined. A friend might e-mail you at work, so you have her in both your contact databases. Then her e-mail address might change, and you update that information in your personal address book but not in your work one. Before long, you have duplicated contacts and out-of-date contacts, and it's hard to tell which is correct. How you include Facebook or LinkedIn messaging in your contact profile is unclear.

In addition to problems keeping all your contact databases current, it can be a hassle to migrate the database from your old phone. Some cellular carriers or firms have offered a service that converts your existing files to your new phone, but it's rarely a truly satisfying experience. You end up spending a lot of time correcting the assumptions it makes.

You now face that dilemma again with your Galaxy S 4: deciding how to manage your contacts. The purpose of this chapter is to give you the information on the advantages of each approach so that you can decide which one will work best for you. That way, you won't have the frustration of wishing you had done it another way before you put 500 of your best friends in the wrong filing system.

Bringing It All Together

Your phone wants you to have the ability to communicate with everyone you would ever want to in any way that you know how to talk to them. This is a tall order, and your Galaxy S 4 makes it as easy as possible. In fact, I would not be surprised if the technology implemented in the Contact application becomes one of your favorite capabilities in the phone. After all, your phone is there to simplify communication with friends, family, and co-workers, and the Contacts application on your phone makes it as easy as technology allows.

At the same time, this information is only as good as your contact database discipline. The focus of this chapter is to help you to help your phone to help you.

So far, you've seen how to make and receive calls, how to make and receive texts, and make and receive e-mails. You've started with an empty contact database. You may have noticed that you have been invited to make the calls and texts that you sent or received into contacts. In this chapter, I cover how to do that.

Using the Galaxy S 4 Contact Database

The fact of the matter is that if you introduced your phone to your e-mail accounts back in Chapter 5, the Contacts list on your phone has all the contacts from each of your contact lists.

Learning the Contact Database on your phone

Take a look at it and see. From your Home screen, tap the Contacts icon.

If you have not created a Gmail account, synced your personal e-mail, or created a contact when you sent a text or made a call, your Contacts list will be empty. Otherwise, you will see a bunch of your contacts are now on your phone, sorted alphabetically like shown in Figure 6-1.

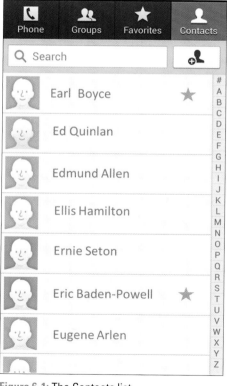

Figure 6-1: The Contacts list.

This database, and the Contacts application that manages the data, does more than just store names, phone numbers, and e-mail addresses. It can include the following information:

- The first and last name of the contact in separate fields
- All telephone numbers, including
  - Mobile
  - Home
  - Work
  - Work fax
  - Pager
  - Other
- E-mail addresses
  - Home
  - Work
  - Mobile
- Up to nine IM addresses, including all the largest IM services (such as Google Talk, AIM, Windows Live, and Yahoo!)
- Company
- Job Title
- Nickname
- Mailing address for
  - Home
  - Work
  - Another location
- Any notes about this person
  - Web address
  - Birthday
  - Anniversary

Finally, you can assign a picture for the contact. It can be one out of your Gallery; you can take a new picture; or as I discuss in Chapter 8, you can connect a social network, like Facebook, which will then use that contact's profile picture.

Fortunately, the only essential information is a name. Every other field is optional, and is only displayed if there is information to be displayed. See Figure 6-2 to see a sparsely populated contact.

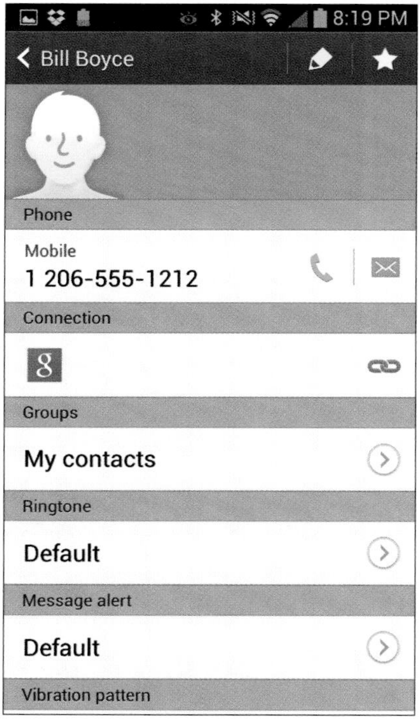

Figure 6-2: A basic contact.

This Contacts list is smart. Allow me to explain some of the things that are going on.

Say your best friend is Bill Boyce. You sent Bill a text earlier to let him know about your new phone. You followed the instructions in Chapter 4 and entered his telephone number. Without instruction, you took it to the next step and tapped Add Contact. You were prompted to add his name, which you did. Now your phone has a contact, "Bill Boyce."

Then you linked your e-mail. Of course your buddy Bill is in your e-mail Contacts list. So while you were reading this chapter, several things happened. First, your phone and your

Gmail account synced. Your phone thinks about it, and figures this must be the same person. It automatically combines all the information in one entry on your phone!

Then your phone automatically updates your Gmail account. On the right side of Figure 6-3, you see the Google logo just beneath the e-mail address. That means that this contact is synced with the Gmail account. You did not have to do anything to make this happen.

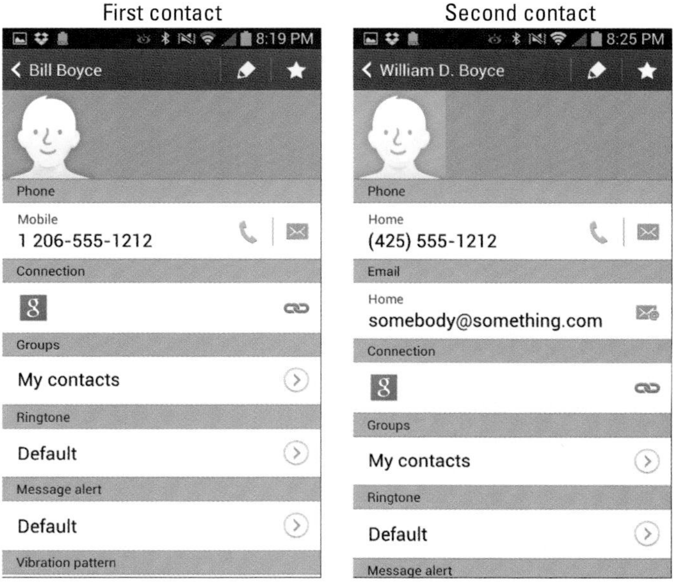

First contact   Second contact

Figure 6-3: Two contacts for the same person.

Your phone noticed that Bill's work number was in your e-mail contact information, but the mobile phone number you used to text him was not. No problem! Now the contact on your phone includes both the information you had in your e-mail contact as well as Bill's cellular phone number.

Linking Contacts on your phone

Now, as slick as this system is, it isn't perfect. In this scenario, both contacts have the same first and last name. However, if the same person has a different name, you have to link these contacts. For example, if you created a contact for Bill Boyce, but your e-mail refers to him as William D. Boyce, your phone will assume that these are two different people.

No problem, though. Do you see the chain links icon in Figure 6-3 in the box that says Connection? Here are the steps to link the two contacts for the same person:

1. **From a contact, tap on the chain icon.**

   This brings up the Joined Contact pop-up.

   Choose the contact whose name you want to be the primary name. For example, I tapped the link on the William D. Boyce contact. That will be the name used on the combined contact going forward.

2. **Tap the Join another Contact button at the bottom of the screen.**

   Your phone will try to help you with some suggestions. This is seen in Figure 6-4. If it gets it all wrong, you can just find the other contact by searching alphabetically.

Figure 6-4: Some linking suggestions.

3. Tap the Contact you want joined.

In this case, the second guess, Bill Boyce, is the one you want. Tap this name. The result is shown in Figure 6-5.

Figure 6-5: The linked contacts.

The combined link has all the information on this person.

Grasping the link between the Contact database on your phone and Gmail

If you created a Gmail account back in Chapter 5, realize that your phone and this account automatically share all the contact information. This happens without you having to do anything. It just works. When you update your phone, the Gmail account automatically updates. When you update your Gmail account, your phone automatically updates.

In addition to being smart, here are some good reasons why you'd want to use your Gmail account to store your contacts, rather than relying on a database stored solely on your phone:

- ✔ You don't lose your database if you lose your phone.

- ✔ If more of your social time is spent on your computer and you use your phone only occasionally, having the database on your computer be the most accurate is probably more valuable.

- ✔ As nice as the keyboard and screen are on the Galaxy S 4, it's easier to make additions, changes, and deletions to a database when you use a full keyboard and large screen. It's your choice.

Keep in mind that your phone stores a copy of all contacts in case you are unable to connect to your Gmail account, but the "official" copy of your contacts is stored away from your phone and safely hosted by your friends at Google.

Entering the Contacts on Your SIM Card

If your previous phone worked with AT&T or T-Mobile, you probably have a SIM card. Figure 6-6 shows a profile of a typical SIM card, next to a dime for scale, although yours probably has the logo of your cellular carrier nicely printed on the card. To the right of the SIM card is the newer micro SIM card. This is the same idea, but in a smaller package.

Figure 6-6: A SIM card and a micro SIM card.

If your cellular carrier was Verizon, Sprint, or US Cellular, you may be confused. Your Galaxy S 4 has a SIM card. What's the story? These carriers use CDMA technology for voice and some data. The phones using CDMA technology and data services up to 3G did not use a SIM card. Today, *all* carriers in the US are implementing a super high-speed data technology called LTE, also called 4G. Because your phone is capable of LTE, you now have a SIM card.

Like many users, you probably have stored your phone contacts on your SIM card. Some GSM-based phones allowed you to store your contacts on internal memory within the phone. This allowed you to store more contacts and more information on each contact than you could on the SIM card. However, in most cases, you probably stored your contacts on the SIM card. I suggest that you move them off and integrate them with your other contacts. Here is how to do this:

1. **From the Home screen, tap on Contacts.**

   You know how to do this.

2. **Tap the Menu key.**

   This brings up the pop-up screen in Figure 6-7.

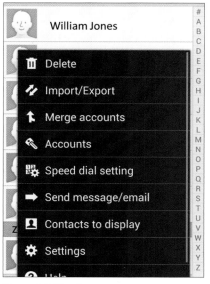

Figure 6-7: The Contacts menu pop-up screen.

These are all the options for Contacts.

3. **Tap the Import/Export option.**

This brings up the screen in Figure 6-8.

Figure 6-8: The Import/Export options.

4. **Tap Import from SIM Card.**

It imports this information, and while you do other things, it syncs everything on your phone and then your Gmail account.

Creating Contacts within Your Database

Your phone is out there trying to make itself the ultimate contact database with as little effort on your part as possible. The interesting thing is that the salesperson in the cellular store did not really explain this to you. It is a subtle but important capability that is hard to communicate on the sales floor. Here is what happens.

Whenever you make or receive a call, send or receive an e-mail, or send or receive a text, your phone will look up that telephone number or e-mail address to check if it has seen it before. If it has, it will have all the other information on that person ready. If it does not recognize that telephone number or e-mail, it will ask if you want to make it a contact. What could be easier?

Adding contacts as you communicate

When you receive a call, a text, or an e-mail from someone who isn't in your Contacts list, you're given the option to create a profile for that person. The same is true when you initiate contact with someone who isn't in your Contacts list. Back in Chapter 3, you saw the dialing screens seen in Figure 6-9.

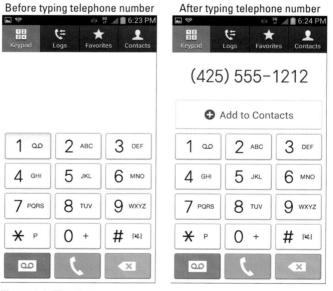

Before typing telephone number   After typing telephone number

Figure 6-9: The dialing screens.

When you tap Add to Contacts, you're immediately given the option to create a contact or update an existing contact. Your phone doesn't know whether this is a new number for an existing contact or a totally new person. Rather than make an assumption (like lesser phones on the market would do), your phone asks you whether you need to create a new profile or add this to an existing profile.

Adding contacts when you are dialing

1. **Tap the Phone icon.**

   When you first bring up the Phone application, it brings up the keypad with a blank screen, as seen in the left screen in Figure 6-9.

2. **Start dialing the number**

   When you start entering the first number, you get a pop-up that asks if you want to Add to Contacts.

   Be patient. As you continue to type, your phone tries to guess whose name you are typing. As shown in Figure 6-10, your phone sees that the digits you have typed are included in the phone number for your good buddy Robert Baden-Powell. As a courtesy, it tries to offer you the ability to save your tapping finger and just call Robert.

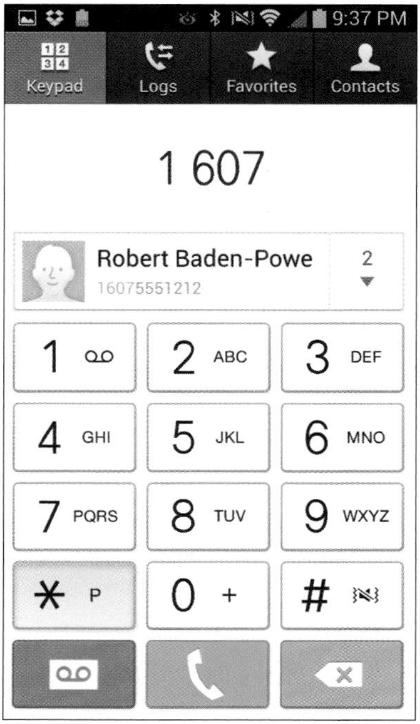

Figure 6-10: The Phone screen as you begin entering the phone number.

If Robert isn't the right one, you can see that there is another person with that number sequence in your Contacts list. If you mean to call the other person and not Robert, you can tap on the 2, and one of these contacts will be called.

However, if you're dialing a new number for the first time, just keep on typing. It will take those digits until it no longer recognizes the number. Eventually it gives up and shows you the screen in Figure 6-11.

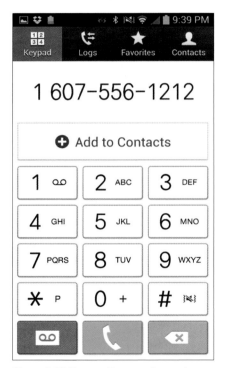

Figure 6-11: Eventually your phone gives up trying to guess an existing contact.

Keep on typing until you have the complete number dialed.

3. **When done typing, tap Add to Contacts.**

4. Tap Save to Phone.

This brings up the option to save it as a new contact or to add this phone number to an existing contact.

5. Tap Create Contact.

An empty contact profile like the one in Figure 6-12 appears.

Figure 6-12: The Add to Contacts option.

Enter as much information on this contact as you want.

6. Tap Save at the top of the screen.

This contact will soon be synced with your Gmail account.

Adding contacts manually

Adding contacts manually involves taking an existing contact database and entering its entries to your phone, one profile at a time. (This option, a last resort, was the only option for phones back in the day.)

1. Tap the Contacts icon.

This brings up the screen shown in Figure 6-13.

2. Tap the + (plus) sign.

A screen with text boxes appears. This is the profile for the contact.

Tap the plus sign.

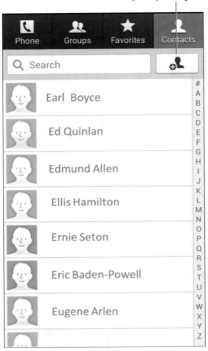

Figure 6-13: The Contacts List screen.

3. **Fill in the information that you want to include.**

   This screen has defaults. For example, it assumes that you want to add the mobile phone number first. If you want to add the work or home number first, tap on Mobile to change the field description.

4. **If you want to add a second telephone number, tap the little green plus sign, and another text box shows up.**

5. **When you are done entering data, tap Save at the top of the screen.**

   The profile is now on your phone. Repeat the process for as many profiles as you want to create.

7

You've Got the Whole Web World in Your Hands

*I*f you're like most people, one of the reasons you got a smartphone is because you want Internet access on the go. You don't want to have to wait until you get back to your laptop or desktop to find the information you need online. You want to be able to access the Internet even when you're away from a Wi-Fi hotspot — and that's exactly what you can do with your Galaxy S 4 phone. In this chapter, I show you how.

The browser that comes standard with your Galaxy S 4 phone works almost identically to the browser that's currently on your PC. You see many familiar toolbars, including the Favorites and search engine. And the mobile version of the browser includes tabs that allow you to open multiple Internet sessions simultaneously.

Starting the Browser

To launch the browser on your Galaxy S 4 phone, tap the Browser icon on one of the Home screens (shown in the following figure). Alternatively, tap the Application icon and then tap the Browser icon.

As long as you're connected to the Internet (that is, either near a Wi-Fi hotspot or in an area where you have cellular service), your home page appears. Your default home page could be blank or the Google home page, but most cellular carriers set their phones' home pages to their own websites or to a site selected by them.

Accessing Mobile (Or Not) Websites

After the browser is up, it's designed to function like the browser on your PC. At any time, you can enter a web address (the URL) by tapping the text box at the top of the screen.

For example, the page seen in Figure 7-1 is the mobile version of the website RefDesk.com.

You can get to this site by entering **m.refdesk.com** into the text block at the top from the software keyboard.

As a comparison, Figure 7-2 shows the PC version of this site. It has many more pictures, and the text is smaller. The mobile version loads faster, but looks less flashy.

RefDesk.com is far from the only website to offer a mobile version of its site. Many sites —from Facebook to Flickr, Gmail to Wikipedia — offer mobile versions.

So how do you get to the mobile version of your favorite websites? If a website has a mobile version, your phone browser will usually bring it up automatically. Samsung has gone out of its way to make the web experience on the Galaxy S 4 similar to what you experience when browsing the web on your desktop.

Figure 7-1: The mobile version of the website RefDesk.com.

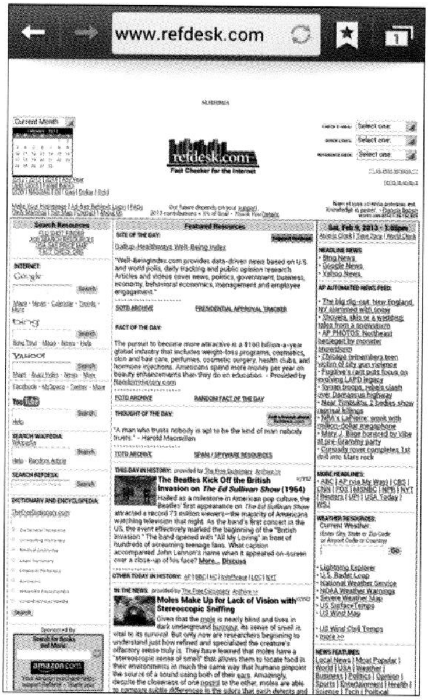

Figure 7-2: The PC version of RefDesk.com.

The most common differences between the address of a mobilized website and a regular one are

✔ **An m instead of www:** For example, the mobile version of `www.refdesk.com` is `m.refdesk.com`.

✔ **/mobile.com at the end of the address:** For example, the mobile version of Amazon.com is `www.amazon.com/mobile`.

When a site doesn't offer a mobile version (or when you just prefer to view the standard version of a particular site), you can stretch and pinch to find the information you need. (Stretch and pinch are hand movements you can use to enlarge/shrink what you see onscreen, as covered in Chapter 2.)

Navigating the Browser

With the browser active on your phone, as shown in Figure 7-3, the following are your options:

Tap for a new window.

Figure 7-3: The open browser.

✔ **New Window:** Tap on the icon in the upper right corner with the 1 on the page. This brings up a screen, as seen in Figure 7-4.

Here are your options:

- If you just want a new window for a second browser section, tap the + (plus) sign. You get a second browser screen.

- If you want to open a new window, but do it without your phone tracking what sites you've visited, tap the icon with a silhouette of a person in a trench coat and their hat pulled down. That brings up an incognito browser session. (Don't tell me why you want to do this. I don't need to know.)

Figure 7-4: The New Window screen.

- If you just want to close an open window, you tap the red – (minus) sign next to the slightly smaller web page. It will disappear.

✔ **Bookmarks:** You can tap the icon seen in the following figure to make this site a favorite. I talk more about bookmarks in the next section.

✔ **Refresh:** Tap to resend data from the active tab. This is useful if there is no activity for a while. This is the same icon as on your desktop browser with the semi-circular arrows chasing each other's tails.

✔ **Back or Forward:** The Back and Forward buttons work just like the browser on your PC.

Using Bookmarks

As convenient as it is to type URLs or search terms with the keyboard, you'll find it's usually faster to store a web address that you visit frequently as a bookmark. Making bookmarks is a handy way to create a list of your favorite sites that you want to access over and over again.

The term *bookmarks* is roughly the equivalent of a Favorite on a Microsoft Internet Explorer browser.

In this section, I tell you how to bookmark a site and add it to your list of favorites. I also tell you how you can see your list of bookmarks.

Adding bookmarks

When you want to add a site to your bookmark list, simply visit the site. From there, follow these steps:

1. **Tap the Bookmark button.**

   This brings up a screen like that shown in Figure 7-5.

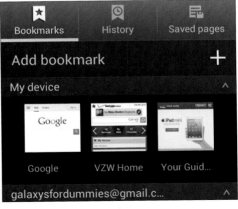

Figure 7-5: The Bookmarks screen.

Chances are that your carrier already put in a number of bookmarks. Some are for popular sites; others help you manage your account. The point is that you can add your own sites.

2. Tap the button that says Add Bookmark.

This brings up a screen like Figure 7-6.

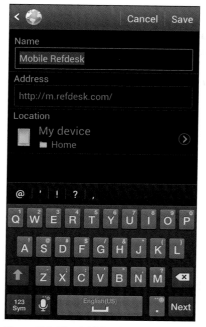

Figure 7-6: The Add Bookmark screen.

The first textbox is the name you want to call the bookmark. In this case, the default is Mobile Refdesk. You can choose to shorten it to just Refdesk, or anything you want to call it. When ready, tap Next on the keyboard.

The second textbox is the web address (URL). You probably want to leave this one alone. Just tap Next again.

3. Tap the Save button at the upper right corner of the screen.

This puts a thumbnail of the website in your Bookmarks file. This is shown in Figure 7-7.

The next time you come to Bookmarks, you can tap this thumbnail, and this page will refresh and come up in its own window.

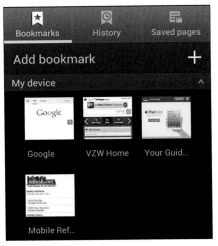

Figure 7-7: The Bookmarks screen with your new addition.

Bookmark housekeeping

Bookmarks are cool and convenient, but you don't always want to save them forever. Rather than have one you no longer want take up prime real estate on your Bookmarks screen, you can delete it. Press and hold the thumbnail of the website you want to delete. This brings up a pop-up like in Figure 7-8.

To delete the bookmark, tap Delete Bookmark. It confirms that this is indeed what you want to do. Tap Yes and it's gone.

On the other hand, say you really like this site. You can make it your home page. Tap Set as Homepage. Boom. Done. It's your home page.

In addition to using bookmarks, you can also put a link on your phone's Home screen. This results in even faster access to your favorite websites.

To put a site on the Home screen of the phone, it must first be stored as a bookmark. From within the bookmark screen in Figure 7-8, tap Add Shortcut to Home Screen. When you return to the Home screen, you'll see an icon with the bookmark's name. When you want to see this web page, all you do is tap this icon, and a browser session opens with this as the web page.

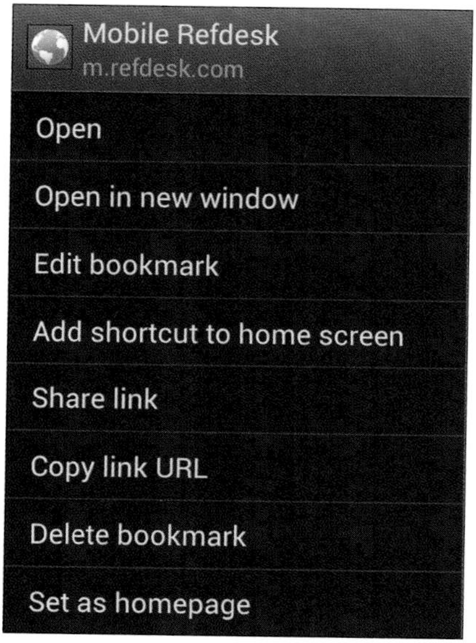

> **Mobile Refdesk**
> m.refdesk.com
>
> Open
>
> Open in new window
>
> Edit bookmark
>
> Add shortcut to home screen
>
> Share link
>
> Copy link URL
>
> Delete bookmark
>
> Set as homepage

Figure 7-8: Bookmark housekeeping options.

Googling Your Way to the Information You Need: Mobile Google Searches

When you open the browser, you can use any search engine that you want (for example, Bing or Yahoo!). Still, some functions — web searches and map searches — work especially well when you use the Google search engine.

At the highest level, the search process works just like on your PC: You type (or tap) in a search topic, press Enter, and the search engine goes and finds it. Depending upon the search engine and your phone, you might even have the ability to speak your search topic aloud (searching by voice).

Android works well with the Google browser primarily because Android was developed by Google.

The Galaxy S 4 phone works to make Internet searches more convenient. Figure 7-9 shows the Google mobile web page.

There are three nondescript bars off to the left that are circled in Figure 7-10. If you tap them, the screen slides to the right.

These searches are all available on Google, but clicking this button makes specific searches for images, videos, maps, and so on even easier to access.

Figure 7-9: The Google mobile web page.

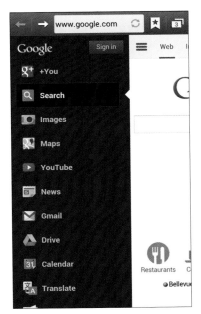

Figure 7-10: The secret Google Search icons.

8

Shopping in the Google Play Store

*O*ne of the things that makes smartphones (like the phones based upon the Google Android platform) different from regular cellphones is that you can download better applications than what comes standard on the phone. Most traditional cellphones come with a few simple games and basic applications. Smartphones usually come with better games and applications. For example, on your Galaxy S 4 phone, you get a more sophisticated contact manager, an application that can play digital music (MP3s), basic maps, and texting tools.

To boot, you can download even better applications and games for phones based on the Google Android platform. Many applications are available for your Galaxy S 4 phone, and that number will only grow over time.

So, where do you get all these wonderful applications? The primary place to get Android apps is the Play Store. You might be happy with the applications that came with your phone, but look into the Play Store, and you'll find apps you suddenly won't be able to live without.

In this chapter, I introduce you to the Play Store and give you a taste of what you find there. For information on how to buy and download apps, keep reading.

Exploring the Play Store: The Mall for Your Phone

The Play Store is set up and run by Google, primarily for the benefit of people with Android phones. Adding an application to your phone is similar to adding software to your PC. In both cases, a new application (or software) makes you more productive, adds to your convenience, and entertains you for hours on end — sometimes for free. Not a bad deal.

There are some important differences, however, between installing software on a PC and getting an application on a cellphone:

- **Smartphone applications need to be more stable than computer software because of their greater potential for harm.** If you buy an application for your PC and find that it's unstable (for example, it causes your PC to crash), sure, you'll be upset. If you were to acquire an unstable application for your phone, though, you could run up a huge phone bill or even take down the regional cellphone network. Can you hear me now?

- **There are multiple smartphone platforms.** These days, it's pretty safe to assume that computer software will run on a PC or a Mac or both. On the other hand, because of the various smartphone platforms out there, different versions within a given platform aren't always compatible. The Play Store ensures that the application you're buying will work with your version of phone.

Getting to the Store

You can access the Play Store through your Galaxy S 4 phone's Play Store application or through the Internet. I cover both of these methods in this section.

The easiest way to access the Play Store is through the Play Store application on your Galaxy S phone. The icon is shown in the following figure.

 If the Play Store application isn't already on your Home screen, you can find it in your Applications list. To open it, simply tap the icon.

When you tap the Play Store icon, you will be greeted by the screen shown in Figure 8-1.

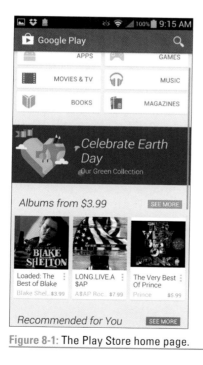

Figure 8-1: The Play Store home page.

As new applications become available, the highlighted applications will change, and the home page will change from one day to the next, but the categories will be consistent over time. These categories are

✔ **Apps:** This showcase highlights valuable applications or games that you might not otherwise come across. This is the first screen that you will see (the left-most screen on the panorama).

✔ **Games:** These apps are for fun and enjoyment. As it happens, these are the most-downloaded kind of applications. Popularity is a good initial indication that an application is worth considering.

Throughout this book, I use the blanket term *applications* to refer to games and other kinds of applications. Some purists make a distinction between applications and games. The thing is, from the perspective of a phone user, they're the same. You download an application and use it, either for fun or to be more productive.

✔ **Music:** You can buy your digital music at the Play Store.

✔ **Books:** Have you been thinking about getting an e-reader, such as a Nook or a Kindle? Before you spend your hard-earned cash, take a look at the book library here and see if you like reading on your phone! If you like the way the Nook or the Kindle work, both are available as applications you can download and use to access your accounts on Barnes & Noble's website or Amazon.com.

✔ **Magazines:** Same idea as with books, only these are for periodicals.

✔ **Movies and TV:** As with music, you can download multimedia files and view your favorite movies and TV shows. You can watch these on your Galaxy S 4's screen or connect to your HD TV.

Seeing What's Available: Shopping for Android Apps

When you head to the local mall with a credit card but without a plan, you're asking for trouble. Anything and everything that tickles your fancy is fair game. Similarly, before you head to the Play Store, it helps if you have a sense of what you're looking for, so you don't spend more than you intended.

The applications for your Galaxy S 4 phone fall into the following subcategories:

- **Games:** Your Galaxy S 4 phone takes interactive gaming to a new level. Games in this section of the Play Store fall into the following categories:

  - *Arcade and Action:* Think of games that are based upon arcades: shooting games, racing games, and other games of skill and/or strategy.

  - *Brain and Puzzle:* Think crossword puzzles, Sudoku, and other word or number games.

  - *Cards and Casino:* Find an electronic version of virtually every card or casino game. (If you know of any game that's missing, let me know so I can write the application and sell it to the three people who play it.)

  - *Casual:* This crossover category includes simpler games, some of which are also arcade, action, or cards, but are distinguished by the ease with which you can pick it up and play and then put down. Solitaire may be the most widespread example of a casual game.

- **Applications:** The "non-games" fall into many subcategories, including these:

  - *Communication:* Yes, the Galaxy S 4 phone comes with many communications applications, but these Play Store apps enhance what comes with the phone: for example, tools that automatically send a message if you're running late to a meeting, or that text you if your kids leave a defined area.

  - *Entertainment:* Not games per se, but these apps are still fun: trivia, horoscopes, and frivolous noise-making apps. (These also include Chuck Norris "facts." Did you know that Chuck Norris can divide by 0?)

  - *Finance:* This is the place to find mobile banking applications and tools to make managing your personal finances easier.

- *Health:* This is a category for all applications related to mobile medical applications, including calorie counters, fitness tracking, and tools that help manage chronic conditions, such as diabetes.

- *Lifestyle:* This category is a catch-all for applications that involve recreation or specials interests, like philately or bird watching.

- *Maps & Search:* Many applications tell you where you are and where you want to go. Some are updated with current conditions, and others are based upon static maps that use typical travel times.

- *Multimedia:* The Galaxy S 4 phone comes with music and video services, but nothing says you have to like them. You might prefer offerings that are set up differently or have a selection of music that isn't available elsewhere.

- *News & Weather:* You find a variety of apps that allow you to drill down into getting just the news or weather that is more relevant to you than what's available on your extended Home screen.

- *Productivity:* These apps are for money management (like a tip calculator), voice recording (like a stand-alone voice recorder), and time management (for example, an electronic to-do list).

- *Reference:* These apps include a range of reference books, such as dictionaries and translation guides. Think of this as like the reference section of your local library and bookstore.

- *Shopping:* These applications help you with rapid access to mobile shopping sites or to do automated comparison shopping.

- *Social:* These are the social networking sites. If you think that you know them all, check here. Of course, you'll find Facebook, LinkedIn, Twitter, Pinterest, and MySpace, but there are dozens of other sites that are more narrowly focused that offer applications for the convenience of their users.

- *Sports:* Sports sites to tell you the latest scores and analysis can be found in this part of the Play Store.

- *Travel:* These apps are useful for traveling, such as currency translations and travel guides.

Many of your favorite websites are now offering apps for your phone that are purpose-built for your phone. I talked in the previous chapter about how you can access websites on your phone. You can use the full site with your high-resolution screen or use the mobile version. A third alternative can be an app that makes it even easier to access the information you want from your phone.

Each application category comes with the applications divided into the following categories:

- **Top Paid:** All apps in this category have a charge.

- **Top Grossing:** These are the apps that are both popular and cost money. This is often a good indication that the app is really good, or at least that it has a crack marketing team. (If the app is not good, the customer comments will show that right away.)

- **Top Free:** None of the apps in this category have a charge.

- **Trending:** Our friends at Google show the applications that are catching on. It is worth considering this category.

- **Featured:** These apps are relatively new, and might or might not have a charge.

In general, you'll probably want to see what you get with a free application before you spend money on it. Many software companies know this, and offer a lower-feature version for free and an enhanced version for a charge. Enjoy the free-market mechanisms on this site and never feel regret for enjoying a free application.

Downloading the Facebook app

To make this process less abstract, I'll show you how to download Facebook for Android as an example.

When you want to add a site to your bookmark list, simply visit the site. From there, follow these steps:

1. **Open the Play Store.**

2. **In the Query box, type** Facebook.

   This brings up a drop-down screen like Figure 8-2.

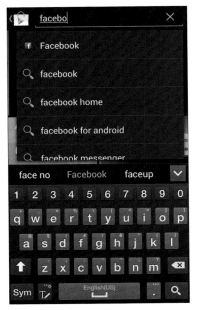

Figure 8-2: The Facebook Search drop-down menu.

3. **Tap on the line with the Facebook icon.**

   You want to get the Facebook *application*, so you can tap the line with the Facebook icon.

   If you tap the line with the Facebook name, it brings up all the titles of apps, games, books, and magazines that include the Facebook name. This screen is seen in Figure 8-3.

   As you can see in the search results, there are several options that include the word *Facebook*. The other lines in the apps section are for apps that include the word *Facebook*. These are typically for apps that "enhance" Facebook in their own ways. As of this moment, there are 112,160 of these. Rather than going through these one by one, stick with the one with the Facebook icon.

When you tap the Facebook app, you get a lot of information, as shown in Figure 8-4.

Figure 8-3: All Facebook Search results.

Figure 8-4: The Facebook app screen in panorama.

Before you continue to the next step, I want to point out some important elements on this page.

- **Title Line:** The top section has the formal name of the application with an Install button. After you click this to download and install the app, you'll see some other options. I give some examples later in this chapter.

- **Screen Captures:** These are representative screens. They are a little too small to read, but they do add some nice color to the page.

- **Feedback Statistics:** This particular app has about 3.5 stars out of five. That's not bad, but not great. The other numbers tell you how many folks have voted, how many have downloaded this app, the date it was released, and the size of the app in MB.

- **Rate and Review:** This is blank until you have downloaded the app that you would be voting on.

- **What's New:** This information is important if you have a previous version of this app. Skip this section for now.

- **Description:** This tells you what the app does.

- **Reviews:** This section gets into more details about what people thought beyond the star ranking.

- **More by Facebook:** The app developer in this case is Facebook. If you like the style of a particular developer, this section tells you what other apps they offer.

- **Users Also Installed:** Play Store tells you the names of other apps that the customers who downloaded this app have also downloaded. It is a good indicator of what else you may like.

- **Users Also Viewed:** Same idea as the previous bullet, but it's somewhat less of an endorsement. The other users only viewed these other apps. They didn't necessarily purchase them.

- **Developer:** This section gives you contact information on the developer of this app.

- **Google Play Content:** This is how you tell the Play Store whether this app is naughty or nice.

4. Tap the button that says Install.

Before the download process begins, the Google Play store tells you what this application plans to do on your phone. This screen is shown in Figure 8-5.

App permissions

Facebook needs access to:

Storage
Modify or delete the contents of your USB storage

Other Application UI
Draw over other apps

System tools
Read battery statistics

Microphone
Record audio

Your location
Approximate location (network-based), precise location (GPS and network-based)

Camera
Take pictures and videos

Your applications information
Retrieve running apps

ACCEPT

Figure 8-5: The Facebook Permissions screen.

This information lists all the permissions you will be granting the application when you download it.

This is similar to the license agreements that you sign. Hopefully you read them all in detail and understand all the implications. In practice, you hope that it is not a problem if lots of other people have accepted these conditions. In the case of a well-known application like Facebook, you are probably safe, but you should be careful with less popular apps.

Back in Chapter 1, you were presented with the option to prevent an app from having access to your location information. I mentioned that you could allow apps to know where you are on a case-by-case basis. Here is where that issue comes up. Each app asks you for permission to access information, such as your location. If you do not want the app to use that information or share it somehow, here is where you would find out if the app uses this information. You may be able to limit the amount of location information. If you are not comfortable with that, you should decline the app in its entirety.

5. **Tap the Accept button.**

Before the download process starts, your app may want to know two things. First, do you want your phone to automatically update when Facebook (or the app provider) releases a newer version? In general, this is the most convenient option. It is rare, but not unheard of that an update makes things worse.

The second is whether you want to wait for the update to take place only when you have a Wi-Fi connection. This prevents your phone from downloading a huge application update over the cellular network. In most cases, using a Wi-Fi connection is a better option. Facebook asks you this question in the pop-up seen in Figure 8-6.

Figure 8-6: The automatic update pop-up screen.

6. Tap OK.

This is like downloading apps to your PC over the Internet. The screens in Figure 8-7 show you the progress of downloading and installing the application.

Download   Installation

Figure 8-7: The Facebook download and installation screens.

This may happen so fast that you look away for a second and when you look back, it's done. Sometimes the Play Store offers you the option to keep on shopping while the app downloads in the background. If you like, you can watch the process in the notification portion of your screen.

Depending upon the speed of your connection, you will see a screen like Figure 8-8.

Apps immediately give you the option to either open them or uninstall.

The Facebook icon is now on your Apps screen along with some other recently added applications, like Angry Birds and Pandora in Figure 8-9.

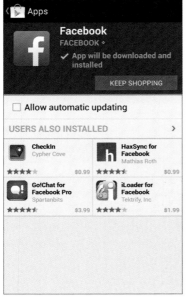

Figure 8-8: The Facebook app screen.

Figure 8-9: The Facebook icon on the Apps screen.

If you want this app to be on your Home screen, press and hold the icon.

Rating and Uninstalling Your Apps

Providing feedback to an application is an important part of the maintaining the strength of the Android community. It's your responsibility to honestly rate applications. (Or you can blow it off and just take advantage of the work others have put into the rating system. It's your choice.)

If you want to make your voice heard about an application, here are the steps:

1. Open the Play Store.

Refer to Figure 8-1.

2. **Tap the Menu button.**

   This brings up a drop-down menu like the one shown in Figure 8-10.

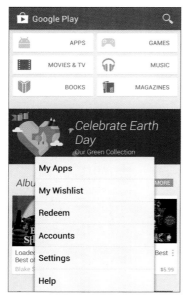

Figure 8-10: The Menu button drop-down menu from the Play Store.

3. **Tap the Line that says My Apps.**

   This brings up the screen, shown in Figure 8-11, of a listing of all the apps that are on your phone. Keep scrolling down. You will eventually see them all.

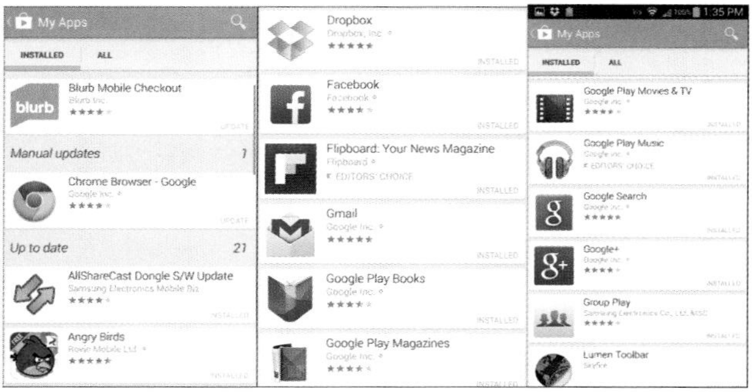

Figure 8-11: The My Apps screen in panorama.

Tap on one of these apps to rate or uninstall it, as shown in Figure 8-12.

If you love the app, rate it highly. You get a pop-up, as shown in Figure 8-13, to rank it and tell the world what you think.

If you hate the app, give it one star and blast away. Then you can remove it from your phone by tapping the Uninstall button.

Uninstall option

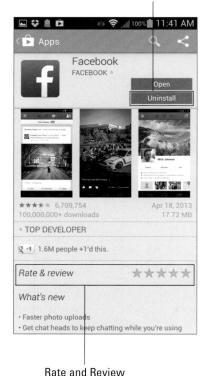

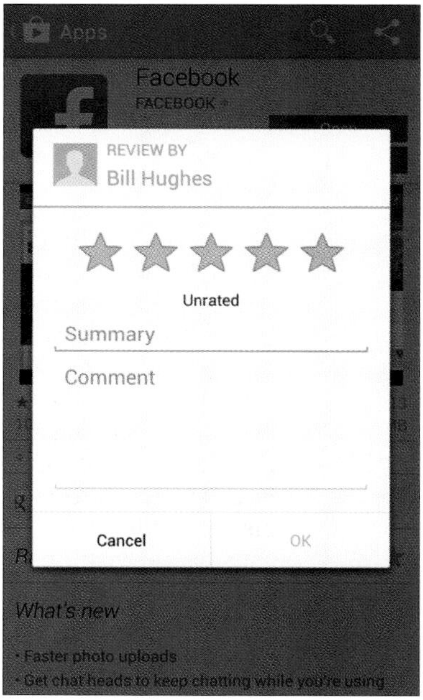

Figure 8-13: The Rating pop-up.

Rate and Review

Figure 8-12: The My Apps page for Facebook.

9

Sharing Pictures and Video

In This Chapter

▶ Taking pictures and video on your phone

▶ Organizing your pictures and video

▶ Sharing pictures and video with friends and family

*I*f you're like many cellphone users, you love that you can shoot photographs and video with your phone. You probably carry your phone with you practically everywhere you go, so you never again have to miss a great photograph because you left your camera at home.

And don't think that Samsung skimped on the camera on your Galaxy S 4. Boasting 13MP of muscle, this camera is complemented with lots of shooting options. Then, you can view your shots on that wicked Super AMOLED screen. Samsung also includes a Gallery app for organizing and sharing. Plus, the camera can shoot stills *and* video.

Stick with this chapter to see how to take a photograph, organize your photos, and share them with friends and family.

Say Cheese! Taking a Picture with Your Phone

Before you can take a picture, you have to open the Camera app. The easiest way is to simply access the Camera application from the Application list. Just tap the Camera icon to launch the app.

A closely related application on your phone is the Gallery, which is where your phone stores your images. The icons for these two apps are shown in the following figure.

With the Camera app open, you're ready to take a picture within a few seconds. The screen becomes your viewfinder. You'll see a screen like the one shown in Figure 9-1.

Figure 9-1: The screen is the viewfinder for the Camera app.

And how do you snap the picture? Just tap the big Camera icon on the right: the camera within the oval. The image that's in your viewfinder turns into a digital image that you can set to either JPG or PNG format.

After you take a picture, you have a choice. The image is automatically stored in another application: Gallery. This allows you to keep on snapping away and come back to the Gallery when you have time.

However, if you want to send that image right away, here's what you do:

1. **From the viewfinder screen, tap the Last Image icon.**

   The viewfinder shows a thumbnail of the most recent image you took. This image is at the bottom right corner of the viewfinder. When you tap it, it brings up the Gallery application. This is seen in Figure 9-2.

The Share button

Figure 9-2: The Gallery app.

This brings up the current image along with the four most recent photos. It also brings up some options. Right now, you're interested in the highlighted Sharing button.

2. **Tap the Share button.**

   This brings up the options you can use to forward the image; see Figure 9-3. These options include any of the following (although your phone might not support all the options listed here).

   - *Messaging:* Attach the image to a text message to someone's phone as an MMS message.

   - *Picasa:* Picasa is a website owned by Google, created to help its subscribers organize and share photos. The main advantage for subscribers is that they can send links to friends or family for them to see a thumbnail of images, rather than sending a large number of high-resolution files. Read more on Picasa in the next section.

- *Email:* Send the image as an attachment with your primary e-mail account.

- *Bluetooth:* Send images to devices, such as a laptop or phone, linked with a Bluetooth connection.

- *Group Play:* This is an application that allows you to share with DLNA and Wi-Fi devices.

DLNA (Digital Living Network Alliance) is a trade group of several consumer electronics firms to create an in-home network among compatible devices. The goal is to make it easier to share music, videos, and photos. Your Galaxy S 4 is DLNA-compliant. If you have other DLNA devices, such as a TV, you can easily share your photos by using the AllShare app.

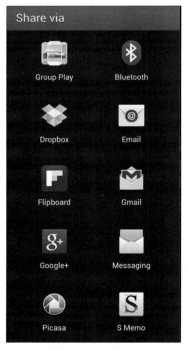

Figure 9-3: Sharing options for the current image.

- *Gmail:* If your main e-mail is with Gmail, this option and the Email option are the same.

- *Facebook:* In Chapter 8, I cover how to connect your phone with Facebook. You can take a picture and post it on your Facebook account with this option. This option appears as an option only after you download the Facebook app and register.

- *Wi-Fi Direct:* Talk about slick! This option turns your phone into a Wi-Fi access point so that your Wi-Fi–enabled PC or another smartphone can establish a connection with you.

- *Dropbox:* Dropbox is the same service that was offered when you first turned on your phone. It's in the *cloud* that everyone is talking about. It works like a hard drive or memory card as far as other apps are concerned, but it's really data storage space on the Internet. A limited amount of space is free for the taking. If you want more space, you can pay a monthly fee.

- *Flipboard:* This is another service that comes as an app pre-installed on your Galaxy S 4. It aggregates your different social networks.

Of course, an account with Gmail (that is, an e-mail address that ends in @gmail.com) is entirely optional. However, there are advantages to having a Gmail account with your Android-based Galaxy S 4 phone: For example, you automatically become a subscriber to Picasa and other Google-owned services.

When you select one of these options, the image is automatically attached or uploaded, depending upon the nature of the service you selected. If one of these options doesn't suit your need to share your pictures, perhaps you're being too picky!

Self-Portrait mode

There are estimates (don't ask for citations) that a big chunk of photos taken with cellular phone cameras are self-portraits. I would have a hard time counting all the images friends on Facebook have sent me that involve someone taking a shot of themselves from their arm's length.

One problem with taking these kinds of pictures is that you cannot be sure that you are centered in the picture. Also, it's hard to be sure that you are pressing the shutter button.

The good news is that your phone has a front-facing camera. All you have to do to take a good self-portrait is tap the self-portrait icon, seen in the following figure. It's in the upper left corner of the viewfinder.

When you tap it, you will suddenly see yourself in the viewfinder! All the settings and options are now at your disposal.

Buddy Share

Your camera has the smarts to recognize your friends from other pictures. Say you tell the camera that a person in one of your images is Fred. Not only will your phone use facial recognition to recognize who is in your picture, but it also makes it easy to share this picture with them by e-mail or SMS text.

You can turn this option on or off from the menu options. When you pull up the menu and tap Buddy Share, a text box appears on the screen next to the faces on the screen. If you tap in one of your contacts, the phone automatically starts looking through your gallery for this individual. It's amazingly good at recognizing your friends!

The Digital Camcorder in Your Pocket

Your Samsung Galaxy S 4 Camera application can also function as a digital camcorder.

Starting the camcorder

All you need to do is to put your camera into Camcorder mode. From the camera viewfinder, you tap the icon with the silhouette of a movie camera in the upper right corner and you switch from photographer to videographer.

At this point, recording video automatically starts. You see the notification that says *Rec* in red text and the time code indicating when it started, as shown in Figure 9-4.

It continues recording until you either tap the Stop button, which is the circle with the dark square in the center on the right side of the viewfinder, or the Pause button, which is the button with the parallel slashes in the middle. If you tap the Stop button, the screen reverts back to the still camera.

Stop

Pause

Figure 9-4: Your phone's camcorder viewfinder.

If you press the Pause button while in Camcorder mode, the buttons to the right morph into the options seen in the following figure. Tap the upper button to switch back to the camera. Your other option is to tap the button with the red dot to begin recording again.

Your phone is not only recording the video, but it's also recording the sound. Be careful what you say!

Taking and sharing videos with your camcorder

Just as you share photos you take with the camera, you can immediately share a video, play it, or delete it by tapping the video viewer. Also, the video is immediately saved on your camera. It is stored in the Gallery app (described earlier in this chapter) or is viewable from your Video Player app.

You can get fancy with some of the settings for your camcorder, but you won't find nearly as many settings as you have for your camera (fortunately!). Two settings, Video Size and Video Stabilization, are available in Settings from the Menu button.

You cannot get to the Settings screen from the Camcorder viewfinder. You must tap the Stop button, which brings you back to Camera mode. From there, tap the Menu button to access Settings.

As with still pictures, you may as well use the highest resolution (or size) unless you're concerned about running out of memory. The highest quality (1920×1080) is the default option, as seen in Figure 9-5.

Use Video Stabilization unless you like the feeling of being seasick.

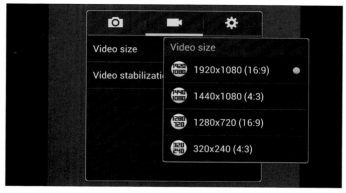

Figure 9-5: The video options.

Under most circumstances, you get the best results by leaving the default settings as they are — unless you want to save memory space by reducing your resolution or get really creative by using black-and-white mode effects. However, in this case, I suggest that you change the default settings and select Video Stabilization.

Deleting an Image

Not all the images on your phone are keepers. This is particularly true if you're using the Continuous option to take a quick series of images.

When you want to get rid of an image, press and hold the image you want to delete. In a second, an icon appears at the top of the screen in the shape of a trash can.

If you want to delete this image, tap Delete. The camera verifies that this is your intent. After you confirm, the image goes away.

When I say that the photos you delete are gone forever, I do mean *for-ev-er*. Most of us have inadvertently deleted the only copy of an image from a PC or a digital camera. That's not a pleasant feeling, so be careful.

Viewing Images on Your Phone

The Super AMOLED screen on your Galaxy S 4 is a great way to enjoy your photos and share them with family and friends. Depending upon the circumstances, you can view images one at time or as a slideshow.

To see one image at a time, just tap that image. See a series of images by tapping Slideshow, which brings up the next image in chronological order, every four seconds. The Slideshow icon is at the top of the image you're viewing.

Sharing Your Photos

Organizing your photos into albums is important. After you've been taking photos for a while, the job of organizing gets more difficult. You can't remember whether that picture of Johnny was from spring break or Easter. Start putting your pictures in albums sooner rather than later!

You can try to do this in the Gallery, but unfortunately, Gallery isn't really set up to handle your entire photo library.

You have a number of options to get the photos off your phone so you can sort, edit, and organize them. I discuss how to do this with a single image at the beginning of the chapter. It's straightforward to do this with multiple images from within a given folder from the Gallery application.

When you tap Share, the pop-up for the Share options appears (refer to Figure 9-3). From this pop-up, you select your sharing option. The multiple images are all handled in one group. *Note:* This is the same list of sharing options you have for a single photo or video.

As I mention earlier, there is much to be said about storing your digital images on the Internet at an image-hosting site like Picasa. If you have a Gmail account, you already have a Picasa account. If not, just register with Picasa at http:// picasa.google.com.

Picasa isn't the only image-hosting site on the block. Flickr and Windows Live Photo Gallery are also available, to name a few. The advantage of using Picasa is that because the Android operating system and Picasa are both owned by Google, Picasa is already integrated into the system. It's not heroic to use the other sites, but that discussion goes beyond the scope of this book.

The advantages of using Picasa include

- **The storage capacity is huge.** You might have a large memory card in your phone, but the storage available on any image-hosting site will dwarf what you have.

- **It's professionally backed up.** How many of us have lost photos? How many of us have lost phones? 'Nuff said.

- **Picasa is free.** Google offers this service at no charge.

- **Access your images wherever you have Internet access.** Although showing pictures on your phone is great, Gallery isn't set up to host your complete photo library. Picasa can.

- **Others can see your images by clicking a link.** Rather than sending the full 8MB image of your kids for each of the 25 images of a birthday party, just send the link.

- **You control who has access.** Picasa allows you to set up access to selected groups. You can set it so that family has more access than your co-workers, for example.

- **You can order prints of images from your PC.** Picasa allows you to order prints from your PC without the need to transfer the images to another storage medium for you to then trudge down to a store to get prints.

- **There are tools to help you sort your images.** Gallery has limited control over your folders. Picasa, in contrast, can get very granular on how you set up your image folder hierarchy. You can get fancy, or you can keep it very simple. Your choice.

Saving to Picasa is easier than sending an e-mail if you have a Gmail account. Tap the Picasa sharing option, and it will upload that image. You can now create a folder to store the image, edit the image, or share it on other web services. All this is as easy as pie!

10

Ten Ways to Make Your Phone Secure

*B*ack in the "old" days, it sure was frustrating to have your regular feature phone lost or stolen. You would lose all your contacts, call history, and texts. Even if you backed up all of your contacts, you would have to re-enter them in your new phone. What a hassle.

The good news is that your smartphone saves all your contacts on your Gmail account. The bad news is that, unless you take some steps that I outline in this chapter, evil-doers could conceivably drain your bank account, get you fired, or even arrested.

Do I have your attention? Think of what would happen if someone were to get access to your PC at home or at work. He or she could wreak havoc on your life.

A malevolent prankster could send an e-mail from your work e-mail address under your name. It could be a rude note to the head of your company. It could also give phony information about an imminent financial collapse of your company to the local newspaper. It could be a threat to the U.S. president, generating a visit from the Secret Service.

Here's the deal: If you have done anything in this book past Chapter 3, I expect that you will want to take steps to protect your smartphone. This is the burden of having a well-connected device. Fortunately, most of the steps are simple and straightforward.

Use a Good Case and Screen Cover

The Samsung Galaxy S 4 is sleek and beautiful. Plus, the front is made of Gorilla Glass from Corning. This stuff is durable and scratch resistant.

So why am I telling you to cover this all up? It's like buying a fancy dress for a prom or wedding and wearing a coat all night. Yup. It is necessary for safe mobile computing.

Speaking from personal experience, dropping a phone on concrete can break some of the innards. The glass may be fine, but the LCD can still crack or the connections become loose. This can happen if you simply keep your phone in a pocket.

There are lots of choices for cases. The most popular are made of silicone, plastic, or leather. There are different styles that meet your needs from many manufacturers. Otterbox is a brand that makes a series of cases made for multiple levels of protection. An example is seen in Figure 10-1.

Figure 10-1: Otterbox cases for the Samsung Galaxy S 4.

You don't just use a good case so you can hand off a clean used phone to the next lucky owner. A case makes it a little less likely that you will lose it.

More significantly, a case protects your phone against damage. If your phone is damaged, you need to mail it or bring it to a repair shop. The problem is that many people who bring their phone in for repair do not wipe the personal information off their device. You really hope that they can pop off the broken piece, pop on a new one, and send you one your way. It is rarely that easy. Typically, you need to leave it in the hands of a stranger for some period of time. For the duration of the repair, those people have access to the information on your phone.

The good news is that most workers who repair phones are professional and will probably delete any information from the phone before they start fixing it.

However, are you sure that you want to trust the professionalism of a stranger? Also, do you really want the hassle of getting a new phone? Probably not, so invest in a good case and screen cover.

Put a Screen Lock on Your Phone

The most basic effort you can take to protect your phone is to put some kind of a screen lock on your phone. If you are connected to a corporate network, they may have a policy on what you must do if you are to access your corporate network. Otherwise, you have eight choices in increasing degrees of security:

- Unlock with a simple swipe across the screen
- Unlock with your face
- Unlock with your face and your voice
- Unlock with a pattern that you swipe on the screen
- Unlock with a PIN
- Unlock with a password
- Encrypt everything on your phone and unlock with a PIN

The first seven options are selected in the Lock Screen option
in Setting. The Encrypt everything on your phone has some
serious implications, so I describe it in the "Encrypt Your
Device" section of this chapter in more detail.

If you want to choose one of the first seven options, here's
what you do:

1. **From the Apps Screen, tap the Settings icon.**

   This should be old hat by now.

2. **Go to the My Device tab.**

3. **Scroll down and tap the Lock Screen option.**

4. **Tap Screen Lock.**

   Each option prompts you through what it needs
   before establishing your security selection.

For reasons that sort of make sense, your phone uses some ter-
minology that can be confusing. To clarify, the term *Screen Lock*
is an option you can select to prevent unauthorized users from
getting into your phone. The term *Lock Screen* is short for the
action of locking your screen or enabling the Screen Lock option.

Preparing for your Screen Lock option

Regardless of what screen lock you choose, I recommend that
you have ready the following choices at hand:

- ✔ A PIN
- ✔ A password
- ✔ An unlock pattern
- ✔ A preference on whether you would like to use a PIN or a
  password

To clarify definitions, a PIN is a series of numbers. In this case,
the PIN is four digits. A password is a series of numbers, upper-
and lowercase letters, and sometimes special characters, and
is typically longer than four characters. A PIN is pretty secure,
but a password is usually more secure. Have them both ready,
but decide which one you would prefer to use.

The unlock pattern is a design that you draw with your finger on a nine-dot screen as shown in Figure 10-2.

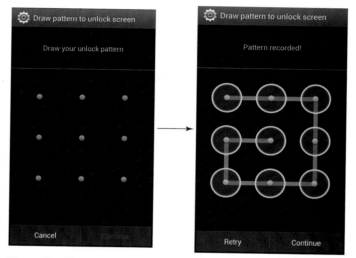

Figure 10-2: The unlock patterns: the blank screen and a sample pattern.

The image on the right in Figure 10-2 shows a sample of a pattern. It happens to include all nine dots. You do not need to use all the dots. The minimum number of dots you must touch is four. The upper limit is nine because you can only touch each dot once. As long as you can remember your pattern, feel free to be creative.

Selecting among the Screen Lock options

The first option, unlocking your phone with a swipe, fools exactly no one and doesn't slow anyone down. Rather than just having the Home screen appear, your phone tells you to swipe your finger on the screen to get to the Home screen. Let's keep going.

The next two options, using facial recognition and using a combination of facial recognition and voice recognition are better, and kind of cool. Your phone has pretty good facial recognition, and most of us bring our faces and voices wherever we go.

That said, these options have some drawbacks. They don't work 100 percent perfectly. The face recognition is imperfect. In addition, your voice can sound different when you are under stress. Finally, it is not always convenient to use voice recognition, like in a meeting or during a movie.

Although these options are cool, I recommend drawing out a pattern as the minimum screen lock option. Then tap on the Pattern option. The phone asks you to enter your pattern, and then asks you to enter it again. It then asks you to enter a PIN in case you forget your pattern.

The next two options on the Screen Lock screen, PIN and Password, are the most secure, but only as long as you avoid the obvious choices. If you insist upon using the PIN "0000" or "1111" or the word "password" as your password, don't waste your time. It's standard operating procedure within the den of thieves to try these sequences first. That's because so many people use these obvious choices.

If someday you forget your pattern, your PIN, or your password, the only option is to do a complete reset of your phone back to original factory settings. All your texts and stored files will be lost. Try to avoid this fate and remember your pattern, PIN, or password.

Encrypting is serious business, so I describe it in more detail in the next section.

Encrypt Your Device

This is the seventh option for protecting your device. This is an exceptionally secure option: It scrambles every file on your phone into gibberish, which it rapidly descrambles when you need it. This sounds great; however, there are some important considerations to think about.

First, all this scrambling and descrambling takes processing power away from other things, like running the apps. This is hardly noticeable in most cases because your phone is awash in processing power. However, you never know when the choice might come back to bite you.

Next, after you encrypt your phone, you can never switch your phone back to non-encrypted. With the Screen Lock options, you can use a PIN for a while, and then switch back to the pattern if you want. Not so with the encryption option. You will never, ever, ever, ever, get it back together.

If you encrypt your phone and then forget your password, your phone is what is called *bricked*. That means that its only use in the future would be in house construction as a brick because you're not going to be able to use it as a smartphone any more.

If you are sure that encryption is for you, here are the steps:

1. **From the Apps Screen, tap the Settings icon.**

   Again, this is old hat by now.

2. **Tap the More tab.**

   This is older hat by now.

3. **Scroll down and tap the Security icon.**

4. **Tap the Encrypt Device option.**

As the screen says, have your password ready, the battery at 80 percent or higher, and set aside an hour when you don't need to use your phone. This time, the password must include at least six characters with at least one number. In this case, the password "password1" is also off the table. This is the second password that thieves routinely try.

Put Your Contact Number on the Screensaver

If you have ever found a lost phone, you are faced with a dilemma with multiple choices. Do you

a. Take it to the local lost and found?

b. Take it to a local retail store for their carrier?

c. Try to track down the rightful owner?

d. Ignore it and not get involved?

Kudos if you do a, b, or c. If you chose c, you hope that the owner has not locked the screen. If you did option b, the store hopes that you have not locked the screen. This allows someone to look at phone calls and texts so that they can contact the owner.

If the screen is locked, like I hope yours is, this plan falls apart. . . unless you have cleverly put your contact information on the screen. That makes it easy to contact you.

Do not use your cellular phone number as your contact number. I hope I do not have to explain why.

Here are the steps to put your contact information on your Lock Screen:

1. **From the Apps screen, tap the Settings icon.**

2. **Tap the My Device tab.**

3. **Tap Lock Screen.**

    This brings up the options shown in Figure 10-3.

< ⚙ Lock screen

Screen security

Screen lock
Swipe

Swipe options

Multiple widgets
Display multiple widgets on your lock screen

Lock screen widgets
Customize your favorite apps, Camera, Clock, and personal message

Shortcuts   OFF
Set shortcuts on lock screen

Unlock effect   ❯
Light effect

Help text   ✓
Show help text on lock screen

Wake up in lock screen
Use wake-up command when swipe unlock is enabled

Figure 10-3: The Lock Screen screen.

4. Tap Lock Screen Widgets.

5. Tap Edit Personal Information.

This brings up the options shown in Figure 10-4.

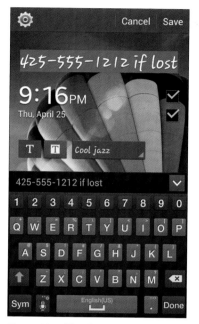

Figure 10-4: The Edit Personal Information screen.

Enter your contact number. This could be a home or work number or an e-mail address, but remember that you don't have much space. After you enter this information, make sure that the Personal Message box on the Lock Screen Widget page is selected and you are set.

If you lose your phone, this makes it easier for whoever finds it to find you. That makes your data safer as fewer people are likely to handle your phone.

Now before you think that you'll never lose your phone, I should point out some research from the firm In-Stat on this subject. They surveyed a panel of more than 2,000 cellular phone users about how often they had their phone lost or stolen. Interestingly, 99 percent of respondents believed that they were better than average at keeping track of their phone.

This shows that almost all of us think we are pretty good at keeping track of our phones. However, this same survey found that the panel lost a phone on average every four years. With about 320 million phones in use across the U.S., that means that more than 200,000 phones "sprout legs and walk away" on a daily basis.

Make it easy to get your phone back by making your contact information accessible.

Be Careful with Bluetooth

Some people are concerned that people with a radio scanner can listen in on their voice calls. This was possible, but not easy, in the early days of cellular. Your Galaxy S 4 can only use digital systems, so picking your conversation out of the air is practically impossible.

Some people are concerned that a radio scanner and a computer can pick up your data connection. It is not that simple. Maybe the NSA could get some of your data that way using complicated supercomputing algorithms, but it's much easier for thieves and pranksters to use wired communications to access the accounts of the folks that use "0000" as their PIN and "password" or "password1" as their password.

Perhaps the greatest vulnerability your phone faces is called *bluejacking*, which involves using some simple tricks to gain access to your phone via Bluetooth.

Do a test. The next time you are in a public place, such as a coffee shop, a restaurant, or a train station, turn on Bluetooth. Tap the button that makes you visible to all Bluetooth devices, and then tap Scan. While you are visible, you will see all the other Bluetooth devices that are out there. You will probably find lots of them. If not, try this at an airport. Wow!

If you were trying to pair with another Bluetooth device, you would be prompted to see if you were willing to accept the connection to this device. In this case, you are not.

However, a hacker will see that you are open for pairing, and take this opportunity to use the PIN 0000 to make a connection. When you are actively pairing, you would not accept the offer to pair with an unknown device. If you are visible, the hacker can fool your Bluetooth and force a connection.

After a connection is established, all your information is theirs to use as they will. Here are the steps to protect yourself:

- **Don't pair your phone to another Bluetooth device in a public place.** Believe it or not, crooks go to public places to look for phones in pairing mode. When they pair with a phone, they look for interesting data to steal. It would be nice if these people had more productive hobbies, like Parkour or searching for Bigfoot. However, as long as these folks are out there, it is safer to pair your Bluetooth device in a not-so-public place.

- **Make sure that you know the name of the device with which you want to pair.** You should only pair with that device. Decline if you are not sure or if other Bluetooth devices offer to connect.

- **Shorten the default time-out setting.** The default is that you will be visible for two minutes. However, you can go into the menu settings and change the option for Visible Time-out to whatever you want. Make this time shorter than two minutes. Don't set it to Never Time Out. This is like leaving the windows open and the keys in the ignition on your Cadillac Escalade. A shorter time means that you have to be vigilant for less time.

- **Check the names of the devices that are paired to your device from time to time.** If you do not recognize the name of a device, click the Settings icon to the right of the unfamiliar name and "unpair" it. Some damage may be done, but hopefully you've nipped it in the bud.

Here's an important point. When handled properly, Bluetooth is as secure as can be. However, a few mistakes can open you up to the human vermin with more technical knowledge than common sense. Don't make those mistakes and you can safely enjoy this capability knowing that all the data on your phone is safe.

Back Up Your Phone

As a responsible user of a PC, I'm sure that you back up your data on a daily basis. That way, if your PC should have a catastrophic failure, you can easily rebuild your system without trouble. (Yeah, right.)

In practice, businesses are pretty good at the discipline of backing up PCs on corporate networks. However, the fact is that most of us are pretty lazy on our personal PCs. Most people back up our PCs only intermittently. I'd be surprised if you ever considered backing up your phone.

You likely have a great deal of valuable information on your phone. Maybe backing up your phone isn't such a bad idea in case it's lost, broken, stolen, or if it has a catastrophic failure. Although much of your information is accessible through your Gmail account, you'll still need to re-build your connections and re-enter your passwords.

Some cellular carriers, like Verizon, offer a backup service preinstalled on your phone: the Backup Assistant. You can access it from Accounts and Sync on your Settings page.

However, have no fear if your phone doesn't come preinstalled with such an application. Many backup services support Android phones in the Play Store.

Protect Against Malware

One of the main attractions for application developers to write apps for Android is that Google doesn't have an onerous preapproval process for a new app to be placed in the Play Store. This is unlike the Apple App Store or Microsoft Windows Phone Store, where each derivation of an app is validated.

Many developers prefer to avoid bureaucracy. At least in theory, this attracts more developers to do more stuff for Android phones.

However, this approach does expose users like you and me to the potential for malware that can, inadvertently or intentionally, do things that are not advertised. Some of these "things" may be minor annoyances, or they could really mess things up.

Market forces, in the form of negative feedback, are present to kill apps that are badly written or are meant to steal your private data. However, this works only after some poor soul has experienced problems — such as theft of personal information — and reported it.

Rather than simply avoiding new apps, you can download apps to protect the information on your phone. These are available from many of the firms that make antivirus software for your PC. Importantly, many of these antivirus applications are free. If you want a nicer interface and some enhanced features, you can pay a few dollars, but this is not necessary.

Examples include NG Mobile Security and Antivirus, Lookout Security and Antivirus, Kaspersky Mobile Security, and Norton Security Antivirus. If you have inadvertently downloaded an app that includes malicious software, these apps will stop that app.

Don't Download Apps from Just Anywhere

Another way to avoid malware is to use only mobile software distribution sites that are trustworthy. This book has focused exclusively on the Google Play Store. There are a number of other reputable sites where you can download Android apps for your phone, including PocketGear and MobiHand.

Keep in mind that these stores are out looking to withdraw applications that include malicious software. Google uses an internally developed solution they call Bouncer to check for malicious software and remove it from the Play Store. Other mobile software distribution companies have their own approach to addressing this problem. The problem is that policing malicious software is a hit or miss proposition.

As a rule, you should hesitate to download an Android application unless you know where it has been. You are most safe by working with reputable companies. Be very skeptical of any other source of an Android application.

Rescue Your Phone When It Gets Lost

Earlier in this chapter, I talked about putting a message on the Lock Screen of your phone. There are also options that allow you to be more proactive than waiting for a Good Samaritan to reach out to your home phone or e-mail.

There are apps that help you find your phone. Here are a few several "lost it" scenarios and some possible solutions for your quandary:

You know that you lost your phone somewhere in your house. You would try calling your own number, but you had your phone set to Vibrate Only mode.

Remote Ring: By sending a text to your phone with the "right" code that you pre-programmed when you set up this service, your phone will ring on its loudest setting, even if you have the ringer set to Vibrate Only.

If you know that your phone is in your house, the accuracy of GPS isn't savvy enough to tell you whether it's lost between the seat cushions of your couch or in the pocket of your raincoat. That's where the Remote Ring feature comes in handy.

You lost your phone while traveling, and have no idea whether you left it in a taxi or at airport security.

Map Current Location: This feature allows you to track, within the accuracy of the GPS signal, the location of your phone. You need to access the website of the company with which you arranged to provide this service, and it will show you on a map the rough location of your phone.

If you have a friend on Latitude, you can call them and get the same information.

Wipe Your Device Clean

As a last ditch option, you can use Mobile Management Software (MMS). MMS software can remotely disable your device or wipe it clean. Here are some of the possible scenarios:

You were robbed, and a thief has your phone.

Remote Lock: This app allows you to create a four-digit pin after your phone has been taken that, when sent to your phone from another cellular phone or a web page, locks down your phone. This is above and beyond the protection you get from your Screen Lock, and prevents further access to applications, phone, and data.

If you know that your phone was stolen — that is, not just lost — do *not* try to track down the thief yourself. Get the police involved and let them know that you have this service on your phone — and that you know where your phone is.

You are a very important executive or international spy. You stored important plans on your phone, and you have reason to believe that the "other side" has stolen your phone to acquire your secrets.

Remote Erase: Also known as Remote Wipe, this option resets the phone to its factory settings, wiping out all the information and settings on your phone.

You can't add Remote Erase *after* you've lost your phone. You must sign up for this kind of service beforehand. It's not possible to remotely download the application to your phone. You need to have your phone in hand when you download and install either a lock or wipe app.

Each of the preceding kinds of applications is available from the Play Store. The simplest security applications are free, but the better quality apps, like the ones mentioned in the antivirus section, are about $10 and require a monthly service fee in the range of up to $5 monthly. Decide what options work for you, consider the price, and protect yourself.

Index

• F •

Facebook, 108–116, 123
facial recognition (security), 135–136
family plans, 11
Favorites, 98
Featured (applications
    category), 109
feedback, on applications, 116–118
Finance (non-game subcategory),
    107
finger navigation motions, 26,
    27–32
flick (motion), 30
Flickr, 6, 129
Flipboard (photo sharing
    option), 123
4G (signal strength), 35
fuel cell charger, 22

• G •

Gallery app, 119–120, 126
Games (on Play Store home
    page), 106
games, downloading, 7–8
gigabytes (GB), 10
Gmail account. *See also* Picasa
    advantages of, 63, 123, 128
    contacts saved on, 131
    required for accessing Play Store,
        62–63
    setting up, 66–69
Gmail icon, 64
Google
    application development, 7–8
    mobile web page, 102
    secret Search icons, 102
Google account, 13
Googling, 101–102
Gorilla Glass, 27, 132
GPS (Global Positioning System), 5
Group Play (photo sharing
    option), 122
GSM (Global Systems for Mobile)
    data technology, 86

• H •

hacking, 141
hardware buttons, 22–26
headset device, Bluetooth, 48–50
Health (non-game subcategory),
    108
high-resolution screen, 4–5, 109
hold (motion), 28–29
Home button, 23, 25–26, 37
Home screen, 14, 32–35
house icon, 34
hyperlinks, 27

• I •

icons
    in book, 2
    on phone, 27
image management application, 6
Image Stabilization setting, 126
images. *See also* photos
    deleting, 127
    storing, 120, 126, 128
    viewing, 128
incoming calls, 46
insides (of phone), 19
In-State (research firm), 139
Internet (primary shortcut), 42
Internet access, 4, 5
Internet searches, 101–102

• J •

JPG format, 120

• K •

Kaspersky Mobile Security, 143
key features, 14
keyboard, 38
Keypad screen, 43
Kindle, 106